THE BOOK OF

PASTA

VOLUME 2

THE BOOK OF

PASTA
VOLUME 2

ANNE SHEASBY

PHOTOGRAPHED BY
PATRICK McLEAVEY

HPBooks

HPBooks
Published by the Berkley Publishing Group
A division of Penguin Putnam Inc.
375 Hudson Street
New York, NY 10014

Copyright © 2001 by Salamander Books Ltd.
By arrangement with Salamander Books Ltd.

A member of the Chrysalis Group plc

Project managed by: Stella Caldwell
Photographer: Patrick McLeavey
Designer: Sue Storey
Home Economist: Alex Winsor
Production: Phillip Chamberlain

First edition: December 2001

The Penguin Putnam Inc. World Wide Web site address is
http://www.penguinputnam.com

This book has been cataloged with the Library of Congress

ISBN 1-55788-375-0

Printed and bound in Spain

10 9 8 7 6 5 4 3 2 1

CONTENTS

INTRODUCTION

Pasta has formed an important part of the Italian diet for centuries, but it is also a very popular food across the world, and is ideal for today's busy cooks. The wide range of fresh and dried pasta is impressive and the shapes and types of pasta readily available ensure that you have plenty of choice when it comes to selecting which pasta to cook.

Pasta also plays an important role in a healthy, well-balanced diet. It is a nutritious food – it is low in fat and provides a good source of carbohydrate and, hence, is a valuable source of energy. Pasta also provides a useful source of protein and some vitamins and minerals.

The word pasta literally means 'dough' or 'paste'. Pasta is made from a basic mixture of durum (hard) wheat flour and water to which other flavorings or colors may be added. A slightly richer type of pasta known as egg pasta or *pasta all'uova* is also commonly available and this is a simple mixture of wheat flour, eggs, water, and sometimes olive oil. Egg pasta tends to be slightly darker in color than the paler basic durum wheat pasta.

The basic pasta dough may then be flavored or colored in various ways and common flavorings include spinach (which colors pasta pale green and is then known as *pasta verde*), garlic and chopped herbs or chopped basil, garlic and chili, tomato paste (pale reddish-orange pasta known as *pasta rossa*), black olives, squid ink (black pasta), mushrooms or porcini (pale brown pasta), beets (which colors pasta deep pink) or saffron (deep yellow pasta).

Whole-wheat varieties of pasta are also available. These are darker brown in color and have a slightly chewier texture. Whole-wheat pasta also contains more dietary fiber than white pasta.

There are also many varieties of filled or stuffed pasta for us to enjoy, including ravioli, tortellini, tortelloni, etc. These include various fillings, ranging from the classic ground meat, spinach and ricotta, or mixed cheese fillings to other flavor combinations such as smoked ham and cheese, or mushroom and ricotta. Again, filled or stuffed pasta are readily available in fresh or dried forms.

Organic pasta is becoming more obtainable, and speciality pasta such as gluten-free or wheat-free pasta including rice pasta, buckwheat pasta, barley pasta, and corn pasta, as well as egg-free and low-protein pasta are also available in health food stores.

An extensive range of both dried and fresh pasta is readily obtainable in many of our supermarkets, delicatessens, and local shops. It is worth visiting a good Italian delicatessen if you can, as they often sell a selection of pasta which is freshly made on the premises.

TYPES AND SHAPES OF PASTA

Pasta comes in a vast array of shapes and sizes, some of which are specific to one type of dish such as cannelloni tubes or large pasta shells (called *conchiglie rigate*) – both of which are ideal for stuffing or filling. You can choose from short pasta such as macaroni or penne or long pasta such as spaghetti or tagliatelle, all of which may be cooked and served in numerous ways.

Some pasta shapes are more suited to particular recipes than others, for example, a chunky sauce is often best served with chunky pasta or pasta shapes such as pappardelle or penne, and a smooth or thin sauce is best served with a long, fine pasta such as spaghetti or capelletti. However, there are no hard and fast rules and it is worth experimenting and choosing for yourself which pasta you prefer. Some of the varieties of pasta you will find are illustrated on page 8.

HOME-MADE PASTA

Home-made pasta is an increasingly popular option and is relatively easy and very satisfying to make. You can make, knead, roll, and shape the dough yourself or you can enlist the help of one of the many pasta-making machines available on the market. To make your own pasta you need very little equipment and once you have mastered the simple technique of making the basic pasta dough, you will find how surprisingly quick and rewarding it is to make and serve to family and friends.

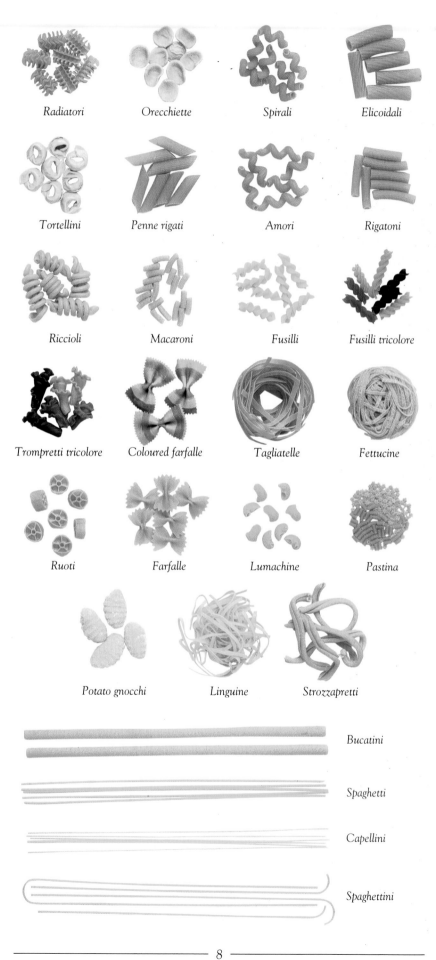

Radiatori

Orecchiette

Spirali

Elicoidali

Tortellini

Penne rigati

Amori

Rigatoni

Riccioli

Macaroni

Fusilli

Fusilli tricolore

Trompretti tricolore

Coloured farfalle

Tagliatelle

Fettucine

Ruoti

Farfalle

Lumachine

Pastina

Potato gnocchi

Linguine

Strozzapretti

Bucatini

Spaghetti

Capellini

Spaghettini

Cannelloni

Lasagne   *Lasagne verdi*

If you decide to make your own pasta on a regular basis, it is well worth investing in a pasta machine which will roll out and cut the dough for you. Home-made pasta can also be made with the help of a food processor or large mixer with a dough hook attachment which easily combines the ingredients to make the basic dough.

Home-made pasta is made from a simple mixture of flour, salt, eggs, oil, and water. The best type of flour to use is known as 'type or grade 00' flour, but white bread flour works equally well. 'Type 00' flour is a very fine textured wheat flour and is available in many supermarkets, delicatessens, or specialist Italian shops. Both 'type 00' and strong white flours have a high gluten content which makes the dough easier to knead, roll out, and shape.

It really is worth experimenting and making your own pasta. Once you have mastered the basic simple techniques, you will thoroughly enjoy making and shaping the dough and you'll never taste pasta quite like it! The flavor and texture of home-made pasta readily repays the small amount of time and effort required to achieve the best results.

The following chapter in this book is devoted to making your own pasta and using the dough to make a variety of tempting plain and filled pasta dishes.

Throughout the remaining chapters of this book, a good selection of dried and fresh pasta has been used to create the wide variety of delicious pasta dishes. Dried and fresh pasta are quicker and more convenient to use than making your own pasta for each recipe and lack of time, especially when cooking a mid-week supper, is often a consideration in our hectic daily schedules. However, if you would like to use home-made pasta for these recipes, do make your own and substitute your home-made pasta for the pasta included in the recipes wherever possible. Refer to the recipes in the first chapter of this book for a general guide to the quantity of lasagne, cannelloni, etc, that the basic pasta recipe will make.

USING A PASTA MACHINE
Both electric pasta-makers and the more popular, compact, hand-turned, rolling type of pasta-making machines are obtainable. Both machines come with different rollers and attachments for cutting and shaping pasta. Always read and follow the manufacturer's instructions when using a pasta machine. Most of them work in a similar way, so these basic guidelines should apply once you have made the dough and rested it (please refer to the next chapter for a basic recipe for home-made pasta).

Divide the dough into equal quantities of dough that you can easily work with – two or four pieces should suffice – and wrap all but one of the pieces in plastic wrap or cover to prevent the pasta from drying out. Press the dough out to flatten it slightly, so that it will fit through the pasta machine. Set the rollers to the widest setting and pass the dough through the rollers to make a strip of dough. Fold the dough in half, press it together, and then pass it through the machine once again on the widest setting.

Repeat this procedure several more times, if necessary, to ensure the dough is smooth and of an even thickness. Then continue to pass the dough through the machine, reducing or narrowing the roller setting each time. Lightly flour the dough if it begins to feel a little sticky.

Use your hands to guide the dough through the machine but do not pull or drag the dough. Finally, pass the dough once through the machine with the rollers set on the narrowest setting. You should now have a long thin strip of pasta. Repeat this process with the remaining pieces of dough.

Place the dough over a pasta dryer (or narrow wooden pole) or on a clean dish towel and leave to dry for a few minutes, before cutting or shaping it. This relaxes the dough and helps to prevent it shrinking when cut. It also makes the pasta easier to cut and prevents the pieces of dough sticking together.

To roll out the pasta by hand, please refer to the directions given in the basic pasta recipe on page 12.

SHAPING PASTA

To make lasagne, simply trim the edges of the pasta sheets, then cut the sheets into lengths to fit the size of your lasagne dish.

Long pasta such as tagliatelle or linguine can be cut either by hand or by using a machine. If using a machine, simply fit the appropriate cutters and pass the pasta sheets, one at a time, through the machine. Hang the noodles over a pasta dryer for a few minutes or spread them out on a clean dish towel, then gather a handful at a time and curl them into small nests before cooking.

To shape tagliatelle or linguine by hand, simply cut the dough into thin strips, or lightly flour the dough and roll up loosely into a jelly roll, then cut into slices using a large sharp knife to the thickness required. Unroll and leave to dry for 5 minutes, then curl into nests before cooking.

Cookie cutters and pastry wheels are useful for cutting the rolled-out dough into decorative shapes. To make filled pasta such as ravioli or tortelloni, please refer to the instructions given in the recipes on pages 14 and 20. Some pasta machines also include a ravioli filler and cutter attachment which makes the job easier.

FLAVORING HOME-MADE PASTA

Many different flavorings can be added to home-made pasta dough. When making the basic dough, try adding 3-4 tablespoons chopped fresh mixed herbs to the flour or a combination of herbs and crushed or finely chopped garlic (about 2 cloves) to make a tasty fresh herb or garlic and herb pasta. Add about 2oz frozen (thawed) chopped spinach to the flour for spinach pasta or *pasta verde*. Add 3-4oz finely chopped pitted black olives to the flour for olive pasta.

Experiment with other flavourings – add the finely grated rind of 2 lemons to the eggs; add 1 tablespoon white cumin seeds to the flour; add 1-2 tablespoons tomato paste, sun-dried tomato paste, curry paste or olive paste to the eggs (you may need to reduce the amount of water used slightly), etc. Try using walnut or chili oil in place of olive oil when making the basic pasta.

Other key ingredients such as olive oil, tomatoes, onions, garlic, and fresh herbs are an important feature in many pasta dishes, adding extra flavor, color and texture and contributing to the overall appeal of the recipe.

Serve cooked plain pasta tossed with a little melted butter or olive oil and add a generous grinding of black pepper and some chopped fresh herbs, if you like. Grated fresh Parmesan cheese sprinkled on top or tossed with the pasta is another simple and delicious way of serving it.

QUANTITIES OF PASTA

For a main meal, allow 3-4oz dried pasta per person or 4-5oz fresh pasta per person. As a general guide, 12oz dried pasta or 1lb 2oz fresh pasta, once cooked and served with a sauce or as part of a recipe, will serve 4 people for a main course. The same quantities apply to stuffed pasta such as ravioli or tortelloni.

COOKING PASTA

Pasta should always be cooked in a large pan of lightly salted, fast-boiling water. Allow a minimum of 9 cups water per 12oz pasta. You can also add a dash of olive oil to the cooking water before adding the pasta – this helps to stop the water from frothing up and over the edge of the pan and also helps to prevent the pasta sticking together. Very large saucepans, pasta pots, or stockpots are the ideal vessels for cooking pasta in.

Once the water has reached a fast boil, add the pasta and stir to separate it. Return the water to a rolling boil, then calculate the cooking time from this moment. Leave the pan partially covered with the lid and stir the pasta occasionally to ensure even cooking and to prevent it sticking together.

Cooking times vary according to the type of pasta used. It is always best to follow the cooking times and guidelines on the package. As a rough guide, dried unfilled pasta usually cooks in about 8-12 minutes and dried filled pasta in 10-15 minutes. Fresh unfilled pasta takes about 2-3 minutes to cook and fresh filled pasta about 5 minutes. The cooking time for home-made pasta is quick and is similar to that for fresh pasta.

Once cooked, pasta should be al dente (literally meaning 'to the tooth') which means the pasta should be just tender but still firm to the bite. Test the pasta frequently while it is cooking and make sure you don't overcook it.

As soon as the pasta is cooked, drain it immediately in a colander or large sieve, shake off any excess water and serve it promptly on warmed plates or in bowls. Always drain pasta thoroughly before serving. Do not rinse pasta unless you are making a recipe such as a pasta salad, where you may rinse the cooked pasta under cold running water to speed up the cooling process.

Also, when pre-cooking pasta sheets or tubes such as lasagne or cannelloni, they should be rinsed under cold running water to prevent further cooking, then drained well, separated, and laid out on clean dish towels ready for use.

You will find that with some pasta, such as dried cannelloni or fresh lasagne, manufacturers' cooking instructions will vary. Some manufacturers suggest pre-cooking the pasta in boiling water for 2-3 minutes, before using it in recipes, while others suggest using the pasta as it is without pre-cooking. To avoid any confusion, if you are using these types of pasta for recipes, always read and follow the basic instructions on the package before making the recipe.

STORING PASTA

Dried pasta, stored correctly in an airtight container in a cool, dry, dark place, will keep for up to 2 years – check the use-by date on the package. Store-bought fresh pasta should be kept chilled. It has a much shorter shelf-life and will keep in the refrigerator for several days, sometimes a couple of weeks, depending on the type – again, check the use-by date on the package and do not eat the pasta beyond this date.

Fresh home-made pasta should be kept chilled and used within a couple of days of making.

Uncooked fresh pasta freezes well and can be cooked from frozen, allowing nominal extra cooking time. Plain cooked pasta does not freeze very well, but dishes such as macaroni cheese where the pasta is coated with a fairly thick sauce tend to freeze quite well. Baked dishes containing pasta such as lasagne or cannelloni also freeze well.

BASIC EGG PASTA

2 cups white bread flour
½ teaspoon salt
2 eggs
1 tablespoon olive oil
1-2 tablespoons cold water

Sift flour and salt into a mound on a clean counter. Make a well in the center and add eggs, oil, and 1 tablespoon water.

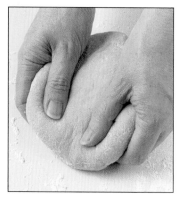

Using your fingers, gradually work all the dry ingredients into egg mixture, adding a little extra water if necessary, to make a soft but not sticky dough. Knead dough on a lightly floured surface for 5-10 minutes or until smooth and elastic. Form dough into a ball, place in a plastic bag and leave to rest at room temperature for 30 minutes, before shaping as required.

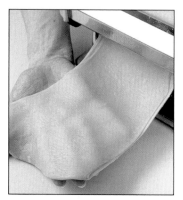

Use a pasta machine to roll and cut the dough (see page 9) or, alternatively, roll out the dough on a lightly floured surface as thinly as possible. Using a sharp knife, cut the pasta into the shapes required. For lasagne, simply cut the pasta into rectangular or square sheets to fit the size of your lasagne dish.

To make tagliatelle, either use a pasta machine to roll the dough, allow it to dry for a few minutes, and then feed the pasta sheets through the machine fitted with the correct cutters. Alternatively, cut the dough into thin strips, or lightly flour the dough and roll up loosely like a jelly roll. Cut into slices to the thickness required. Unroll and leave to dry for 5 minutes before cooking. Home-made pasta should be left to dry for 5-10 minutes before cooking. Spread it out on a clean dish towel or hang it over a pasta dryer or wooden pole to dry out.

Fresh pasta only takes a few minutes to cook; for example, fresh tagliatelle or spaghetti will only take 2-3 minutes to cook. Cook pasta in plenty of lightly salted, fast-boiling water in a large saucepan or pasta pan. Partially cover the pan and give the pasta an occasional stir during cooking. When it is cooked, the pasta will rise to the top of the cooking liquid. Drain thoroughly and serve immediately.

Home-made pasta can also be made using a food processor. Simply sift the flour and salt into the food processor bowl, then add the eggs, oil, and 1 tablespoon water. Process until the dough just begins to come together, adding a little extra water if necessary, to form a soft but not sticky dough. Gather the dough together, wrap and rest as above.

THREE-CHEESE RAVIOLI

1 quantity Basic Egg Pasta dough (see page 12)
½ cup ricotta cheese
scant 1 cup pecorino cheese, finely grated
½ cup finely grated fresh Parmesan cheese, plus
  extra, to serve
1 extra large egg, beaten
freshly ground black pepper
extra beaten egg, for brushing
¼ cup butter, melted, to serve
flat-leaf parsley sprigs, to garnish

Make the pasta dough as described on page 12 and leave to rest for 30 minutes.

Put ricotta, pecorino and Parmesan cheeses in a bowl, with egg and black pepper, and mix well. Divide pasta dough in half and roll out each piece of dough as thinly as possible on a lightly floured surface. Cut each pasta sheet into 2-inch rounds using a cookie cutter. Spoon small mounds of cheese filling into the center of the rounds, brush edges with beaten egg, then fold dough over filling to make a semi-circle. Press edges firmly together to seal.

Transfer to a lightly floured dish towel and leave to rest and dry out for 20 minutes. Bring a large saucepan of lightly salted water to a boil. Add ravioli and cook for 3-5 minutes, or until ravioli is tender and rises to the surface. Drain well and toss with melted butter and extra freshly ground black pepper. Sprinkle with Parmesan cheese and serve garnished with parsley sprigs. Serve with a mixed baby leaf salad.

Serves 4

———— SPICY BEEF RAVIOLI ————

1 quantity Basic Egg Pasta dough (see page 12)
1 tablespoon olive oil, plus extra to serve
1 shallot, finely chopped
1 small fresh red chili, seeded and finely chopped
1 clove garlic, crushed
1 teaspoon ground coriander
1 teaspoon ground cumin
4oz cooked beef, ground
2oz prosciutto, finely chopped
1 tablespoon tomato paste
1 egg, beaten
2 tablespoons fresh bread crumbs
salt and freshly ground black pepper
herb sprigs, to garnish

Make pasta dough as described on page 12 and leave to rest for 30 minutes. Heat oil in a saucepan, add shallot, chili, and garlic and cook gently for 5 minutes, stirring occasionally. Add ground spices and cook for 1 minute, stirring. Add beef and cook gently for 2 minutes, stirring. Remove pan from heat, add prosciutto, tomato paste, egg, bread crumbs, and salt and pepper, and mix well. Divide pasta dough in half and roll out each piece of dough as thinly as possible on a lightly floured surface to form a large square.

Cut each sheet into 2-inch squares using a knife or pastry wheel. Spoon small mounds of beef filling on to squares, dampen edges, then fold to make a triangle. Press edges firmly together to seal. Transfer to a lightly floured, clean dish towel and leave to rest for 20 minutes. Bring a large saucepan of lightly salted water to a boil. Cook ravioli for 3-5 minutes, or until ravioli is tender and rises to the surface. Drain well and toss with a little olive oil and black pepper. Garnish with herb sprigs.

Serves 4

— BEEF & MUSHROOM LASAGNE —

1 quantity Basic Egg Pasta dough (see page 12)
1 tablespoon olive oil
2 red onions, chopped
2 cloves garlic, crushed
1lb 2oz lean ground beef
12oz mushrooms, sliced
2¼ cups passata (sieved tomatoes)
2 tablespoons tomato paste
2 tablespoons chopped fresh mixed herbs
salt and freshly ground black pepper
1lb 2oz fresh spinach leaves, washed
3 tablespoons butter
⅓ cup all-purpose flour
2½ cups milk
1 cup grated pecorino cheese
¼ cup finely grated fresh Parmesan cheese

Make pasta dough as described on page 12. Leave to rest for 30 minutes. Meanwhile, make filling. Heat oil in a saucepan, add onions and garlic, and cook for 3 minutes, stirring occasionally. Add beef and cook until browned all over. Add mushrooms, passata, tomato paste, herbs, and salt and pepper, and mix well. Bring to boil, cover, and simmer for 30 minutes, stirring occasionally. Uncover, increase the heat slightly and cook for a further 10-15 minutes to thicken the sauce slightly.

Preheat the oven to 375F (190C). Lightly grease an ovenproof lasagne dish or baking tin. Put spinach in a large saucepan with just the water that clings to its leaves. Cover and cook for 3-4 minutes, or until just wilted. Drain well and press out excess water. Chop and season with salt and pepper.

Put butter, flour, and milk in a saucepan. Heat gently, whisking continuously, until sauce is thickened and smooth. Simmer for 3 minutes, stirring. Remove pan from heat, whisk in pecorino cheese, and season to taste. Cover sauce closely with parchment paper and set aside. Roll out pasta dough thinly on a lightly floured surface. Cut into 9 rectangles each about 6x4in.

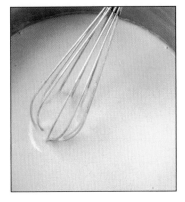

Cook lasagne sheets in batches in a large pan of lightly salted boiling water for 2 minutes. Drain, refresh under cold running water, then drain again on paper towels. Spoon one-third of meat sauce into prepared dish, then top with one-third of spinach. Top this with 3 sheets of lasagne.

Continue layering in this way ending with a layer of lasagne. Pour cheese sauce evenly over lasagne. Sprinkle with Parmesan. Bake for 35-40 minutes until golden and bubbling. Serve with hot garlic bread and a side salad.

Serves 4-6

VARIATIONS: Use lean ground lamb or pork in place of beef. Use sliced zucchini in place of mushrooms.

— MUSHROOM CANNELLONI —

1 quantity Basic Egg Pasta dough (see page 12)
3 tablespoons butter
1 tablespoon olive oil
1 leek, washed and finely chopped
8oz cremini mushrooms, finely chopped
1 zucchini, finely chopped
1¾ cups grated Cheddar or pecorino cheese
1 egg, beaten
1 teaspoon mushroom catsup
1 tablespoon chopped fresh parsley
1 teaspoon chopped fresh tarragon
salt and freshly ground black pepper
2 tablespoons all-purpose flour
1¼ cups milk
herb sprigs, to garnish

Make pasta dough as described on page 12 and leave to rest for 30 minutes. Preheat the oven to 350F (180C). Lightly grease a shallow ovenproof dish or baking pan. Meanwhile, make filling. Heat 2 tablespoons butter and the oil in a pan until butter has melted. Add leek, mushrooms, and zucchini, and cook over a fairly high heat for 5 minutes, stirring occasionally.

Remove pan from heat, cool slightly, then drain off any excess liquid. Add ¾ cup Cheddar or pecorino, the egg, catsup, chopped herbs, and salt and pepper, and mix well. Set aside. Make cheese sauce. Melt remaining butter in a pan, add flour, and cook gently for 1 minute, stirring.

Gradually whisk in milk, then heat gently, whisking continuously, until sauce is thickened and smooth. Simmer gently for 2 minutes, stirring. Remove pan from heat, stir in half remaining cheese, season with salt and pepper, cover closely with parchment paper and set aside.

Roll out pasta dough very thinly on lightly floured surface and cut into 12 even rectangles, each about 6x4 inches. Cook pasta sheets in batches in a large pan of lightly salted boiling water for 3 minutes. Remove from pan using a slotted spoon, refresh under cold running water, then drain on paper towels. Spoon mushroom filling mixture along width of each pasta sheet, then roll them up to make filled cannelloni tubes.

Arrange filled tubes, seam-side down, in prepared dish. Pour sauce over and sprinkle with remaining cheese. Bake for 35-40 minutes, or until golden and bubbling. Garnish with herb sprigs and serve with crusty French bread.

Serves 4

VARIATION: Use fresh wild mushrooms in place of cremini mushrooms. Use chopped fresh sage or rosemary in place of tarragon.

— HAM & CHEESE TORTELLONI —

1 quantity Basic Egg Pasta dough (see page 12)
4oz lean smoked ham, finely chopped
1oz Parma ham, finely chopped
¼ cup ricotta cheese
¼ cup finely grated fresh Parmesan cheese
1 egg
salt and freshly ground black pepper
¼ cup butter, diced, to serve
chopped fresh flat-leaf parsley, to garnish

Make pasta dough as described on page 12 and leave to rest for 30 minutes. Make the filling. Put both hams, ricotta and Parmesan cheeses, egg, and salt and pepper in a bowl and mix thoroughly. Set aside.

Divide pasta dough in half and roll out each piece of dough very thinly on a lightly floured surface. Cut dough into rounds using a 2-inch cookie cutter. Spoon a little filling on to each dough round, brush the edges with a little water, and fold over to make a semi-circle, pressing the edges firmly together to seal. Wrap each filled pasta shape around your little finger and cross the ends over, pinching them together. Slide off your finger on to a floured surface and leave to dry for 20 minutes.

Cook pasta in a large saucepan of lightly salted boiling water for 3-5 minutes, or until tender. Drain thoroughly in a colander, then return to the rinsed-out pan. Add diced butter and freshly ground black pepper and toss to coat all over. Sprinkle with chopped parsley to garnish, then serve with warm ciabatta bread.

Serves 4

VARIATION: Use finely grated pecorino or Cheddar cheese in place of ricotta cheese.

— POTATO & HERB GNOCCHI —

1½lb peeled potatoes, diced
¼ cup plus 4 teaspoons finely grated fresh Parmesan
  cheese, plus extra to serve
⅓ cup butter
1 egg, beaten
1 tablespoon chopped fresh flat-leaf parsley
1 tablespoon chopped fresh basil
1 tablespoon chopped fresh oregano or marjoram
salt and freshly ground black pepper
1¾ cups all-purpose flour
1-2 cloves garlic, crushed
herb sprigs, to garnish

Cook potatoes in a saucepan of boiling
water for 10-15 minutes, or until tender.

Drain well, then return to the pan and mash
until smooth. Add Parmesan cheese,
2 tablespoons butter, the egg, chopped
herbs, and salt and pepper, and beat until
smooth and well mixed. Add half the flour
and mix well, then gradually add remaining
flour, mixing until dough is smooth, even,
and slightly sticky. Shape dough into small
balls, press a fork into top surface of each
ball to flatten slightly and leave an
impression.

Place gnocchi on a lightly floured plate and
chill for 30 minutes. Cook in batches in a
large saucepan of lightly salted boiling water
for 4-5 minutes. Remove from pan using a
slotted spoon, drain well, and keep hot. Melt
remaining butter in a saucepan, add garlic and
cook gently for 2 minutes, stirring. Pour butter
over gnocchi and toss to coat. Sprinkle with
grated Parmesan cheese, garnish with herb
sprigs, and serve with a mixed green salad.

Serves 4-6

—— TOMATO & LENTIL SOUP ——

⅔ cup dried green or brown lentils
1 bay leaf
1 tablespoon olive oil
1 large red onion, chopped
1 clove garlic, crushed
2¼lb plum tomatoes, chopped
1 tablespoon sun-dried tomato paste
3¾ cups vegetable stock
½ teaspoon superfine sugar
salt and freshly ground black pepper
⅓ cup dried mini pasta shapes such as conchigliette
    rigate
3 tablespoons chopped fresh flat-leaf parsley
a little crème fraîche and herb sprigs, to garnish

Cook lentils in a large saucepan of boiling water with bay leaf for 30-40 minutes, or until tender. Rinse, drain, and set aside. Discard bay leaf. Heat oil in a large saucepan, add onion and garlic, and cook for 5 minutes, stirring occasionally, until softened. Stir in tomatoes, tomato paste, stock, sugar, and salt and pepper. Bring to a boil, then reduce the heat, cover, and simmer for 25 minutes, stirring occasionally. Remove pan from the heat and cool slightly.

Puree soup in a blender or food processor until smooth, then pass mixture through a sieve into rinsed-out pan. Discard contents of sieve. Stir pasta into soup and bring gently to a boil. Cover and simmer for 10-15 minutes, stirring occasionally, until pasta is cooked. Stir in lentils and chopped parsley and reheat gently until hot. Ladle into warmed soup bowls to serve. Garnish with a swirl of crème fraîche and herb sprigs. Serve with crusty fresh bread.

Serves 4

– ROAST TOMATO PASTA SOUP –

2lb tomatoes, cut in half
3 tablespoons olive oil
2 onions, chopped
2 cloves garlic, finely chopped
4½ cups vegetable stock
1 tablespoon tomato paste
salt and freshly ground black pepper
⅔ cup dried tubettini or mini macaroni
8 small slices of French stick
½ cup finely grated Gruyère cheese
3 tablespoons chopped fresh basil
basil sprigs, to garnish

Preheat oven to 350F (180C). Put tomatoes in a single layer, cut-side-up, in an ovenproof dish. Drizzle with 2 tablespoons of the oil. Roast for 40 minutes or until soft. Set aside. Heat remaining oil in a saucepan, add onions and garlic, and sauté for 5 minutes or until soft. Stir in tomatoes, stock, tomato paste, and salt and pepper. Bring to a boil, reduce heat, cover, and simmer for 20 minutes, stirring occasionally. Cool slightly. Puree soup in a blender or food processor, then pass through a sieve into rinsed-out pan. Discard contents of sieve.

Add pasta to soup and bring gently to a boil. Cover and simmer for 10-15 minutes, stirring occasionally, until pasta is cooked. Meanwhile, make croutons. Preheat broiler to high. Toast bread slices on one side, then turn them over and top each one with some grated Gruyère. Broil until cheese is melted and bubbling. Stir chopped basil into soup, then ladle into warmed soup bowls. Serve topped with hot Gruyère croutons and garnish with basil sprigs.

Serves 4

PASTA & BEAN SOUP

1 tablespoon olive oil
2 leeks, washed and sliced
2 sticks celery, chopped
2 carrots, thinly sliced
8oz rutabaga, diced
1 bulb fennel, diced
14oz can chopped tomatoes
6¼ cups vegetable stock
salt and freshly ground black pepper
14oz can flageolet or cannellini beans, rinsed and
    drained
¾ cup dried lumachine
2-3 tablespoons chopped fresh cilantro
cilantro sprigs, to garnish

Heat oil in a large saucepan, add leeks and celery, and cook gently for 5 minutes, stirring occasionally. Add carrots, rutabaga, fennel, tomatoes, stock, and salt and pepper and stir to mix. Bring to a boil, then reduce heat, cover, and simmer for 20 minutes, stirring occasionally.

Stir in beans and pasta and return to the boil. Cover and simmer for a further 10-15 minutes, stirring occasionally, until pasta is cooked. Stir in chopped cilantro, and ladle into warmed soup bowls to serve. Garnish with cilantro sprigs and serve with fresh bread rolls.

Serves 4-6

VARIATIONS: Use turnip, celeriac, or parsnips in place of rutabaga. Use chopped fresh parsley or basil in place of cilantro.

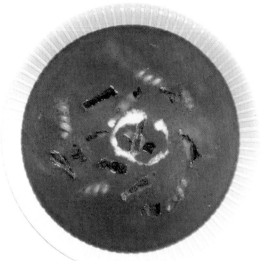

—— SPINACH & STILTON SOUP ——

2 tablespoons butter
1 onion, chopped
3 sticks celery, finely chopped
3¾ cups vegetable stock
1¼ cups milk
salt and freshly ground black pepper
1lb fresh spinach, washed and shredded
⅔ cup dried mini pasta shapes such as fusillini
4 slices rindless smoked bacon
5oz Stilton cheese, crumbled

Melt butter in a large saucepan, add onion and celery, and cook for 8 minutes, stirring occasionally.

Stir in stock, milk, and salt and pepper. Bring to a boil, then reduce heat, cover, and simmer for 10 minutes, stirring occasionally. Add spinach and simmer gently for 10 minutes or until spinach is tender. Remove pan from heat and cool slightly, then puree in a blender or food processor until smooth. Return soup to rinsed-out pan, add pasta, bring to a boil, and simmer for a further 10-15 minutes, stirring occasionally, until pasta is cooked.

Meanwhile, preheat broiler to high. Broil bacon for 3-4 minutes, turning once, until crisp. Drain on paper towels and set aside. Stir Stilton into soup and heat gently until cheese has melted and soup is hot. Ladle into warmed soup bowls. Chop or crumble bacon and sprinkle over soup. Serve with crusty fresh bread.

Serves 4-6

VARIATION: Use other blue cheese such as Gorgonzola in place of Stilton.

— CHICKEN PASTA SOUP —

1lb 2oz skinless chicken thigh fillets
1 onion, chopped
1 clove garlic, crushed
2 sticks celery, chopped
2 carrots, thinly sliced
salt and freshly ground black pepper
2 leeks, washed and thinly sliced
¾ cup quick-cook dried macaroni
4 tablespoons crème fraîche (optional)
2 tablespoons chopped fresh parsley
parsley sprigs, to garnish

Put chicken thigh fillets, onion, garlic, celery, carrots, and salt and pepper in a large saucepan and add 5 cups water.

Bring to a boil and remove and discard any scum that rises to the surface. Reduce heat, cover, and simmer for 45 minutes. Lift out chicken using a slotted spoon and break into smaller pieces, then return chicken to soup.

Stir in leeks and pasta and return to a boil. Cover and simmer for a further 10-15 minutes, stirring occasionally, until pasta is cooked. Stir in crème fraîche, if using, and chopped parsley, then ladle into warmed soup bowls. Garnish with parsley sprigs, and serve with fresh, soft bread rolls.

Serves 4-6

VARIATION: Use chopped fresh cilantro in place of parsley.

MINESTRONE

2 tablespoons olive oil
1 onion, finely chopped
1 clove garlic, crushed
2 sticks celery, finely chopped
2 carrots, finely diced
1 leek, washed and sliced
2oz rindless bacon slices, chopped
5½ cups vegetable or beef stock
14oz can chopped tomatoes
1 tablespoon tomato paste
2 teaspoons dried herbes de Provence
14oz can cannellini beans, rinsed and drained
⅓ cup small dried pasta shapes such as tubettini or
    farfalline
salt and freshly ground black pepper
freshly grated Parmesan cheese, to serve

Heat oil in a large saucepan, add onion and
garlic, and cook gently for 5 minutes,
stirring occasionally. Add celery, carrots,
leek, and bacon and cook for a further
5 minutes.

Stir in stock, tomatoes, tomato paste, herbs,
beans, pasta, and salt and pepper. Bring to a
boil, then reduce heat, cover, and simmer
for 25-30 minutes, stirring occasionally,
until pasta and vegetables are cooked. Ladle
into warmed soup bowls, and sprinkle with
freshly grated Parmesan cheese. Serve with
warm ciabatta bread.

Serves 4-6

—— SPICY SAUSAGE SOUP ——

1 tablespoon olive oil
1 large onion, thinly sliced
1 clove garlic, crushed
2 zucchini, diced
6oz cooked chorizo sausage, thinly sliced
⅓ cup dried pastina (tiny soup pasta)
   or mennucci (little stars)
4½ cups vegetable stock
1 tablespoon tomato paste
salt and freshly ground black pepper
2-3 tablespoons chopped fresh flat-leaf parsley
crisp croutons and fresh Parmesan cheese shavings,
   to serve

Heat oil in a large saucepan, add onion and garlic, and cook gently for 10 minutes, stirring occasionally, until softened. Stir in zucchini, chorizo, pasta, stock, tomato paste, and salt and pepper. Bring to a boil, then reduce heat, cover, and simmer for 10-15 minutes, stirring occasionally, until vegetables and pasta are cooked.

Stir in the parsley and ladle into warmed soup bowls. Sprinkle with crisp croutons and shavings of Parmesan cheese, just before serving. Serve with crusty French bread.

Serves 4

VARIATION: Use 10oz sliced cremini mushrooms or button mushrooms in place of zucchini.

— BEEF BROTH WITH SHALLOTS —

1 tablespoon sunflower oil
8 shallots, thinly sliced
6oz button mushrooms, sliced
5 cups good home-made beef stock
salt and freshly ground black pepper
¾ cup dried lumachine
1 tablespoon chopped fresh parsley
1 tablespoon chopped fresh marjoram or oregano
herb sprigs, to garnish

Heat oil in a large saucepan, add the shallots, and cook gently for 5 minutes, stirring occasionally.

Add mushrooms, and cook for a further 2 minutes. Stir in stock, and salt and pepper. Bring to a boil, then reduce heat, cover, and simmer for 10 minutes, stirring occasionally.

Stir in pasta, cover, and simmer for a further 10-15 minutes, stirring occasionally, until vegetables and pasta are cooked. Stir in chopped herbs, then ladle into warmed soup bowls. Garnish with herb sprigs, and serve with soft bread rolls.

Serves 4

VARIATION: Use 1 large onion, finely chopped, in place of shallots.

CREAMY MUSSEL SOUP

4½lb fresh mussels in shells, cleaned
2½ cups fish or vegetable stock
scant ½ cup dry white wine
1 small onion, cut into quarters
1 bouquet garni
2 tablespoons butter
2 leeks, washed and thinly sliced
2 sticks celery, finely chopped
⅔ cup dried conchigliette
salt and freshly ground black pepper
⅔ cup heavy cream
1 tablespoon chopped fresh parsley
1 tablespoon chopped fresh dill

Put mussels in a large saucepan with stock, wine, onion, and bouquet garni. Cover, bring to a boil, and cook for 4-5 minutes, shaking pan occasionally, until mussels open. Strain mussels, reserving liquid and mussels separately. Discard any mussels whose shells have not opened. Discard onion and bouquet garni. Remove most of mussels from their shells, but reserve a few for garnish. Set aside. Melt butter in a clean saucepan, add leeks and celery, and cook gently for 5 minutes, stirring occasionally, until softened.

Stir in reserved strained stock, pasta, and salt and pepper. Bring to a boil, then reduce heat, cover, and simmer for 10-15 minutes, stirring occasionally, until pasta is cooked. Stir in shelled mussels, cream, and chopped herbs, and heat gently until hot, stirring. Ladle into warmed soup bowls and garnish with reserved mussels in their shells. Serve with warm crusty bread.

Serves 4-6

SPAGHETTI BOLOGNESE

1 tablespoon olive oil
2 onions, chopped
1 carrot, finely chopped
2 sticks celery, finely chopped
1 clove garlic, crushed
1lb 2oz lean ground beef
1 tablespoon all-purpose flour
8oz cremini mushrooms, sliced
14oz can chopped tomatoes
1 tablespoon tomato paste
1¼ cups beef or vegetable stock
1¼ cups red wine
2 teaspoons dried Italian herb seasoning
salt and freshly ground black pepper
12oz dried spaghetti
freshly grated Parmesan cheese, to serve

Heat oil in a large saucepan, add onions, carrot, celery, and garlic, and cook for 5 minutes, stirring occasionally. Add ground beef and cook, stirring occasionally, until meat is browned all over. Add flour and cook for 1 minute, stirring. Add mushrooms, tomatoes, tomato paste, stock, wine, herbs, and salt and pepper, and stir to mix. Bring to a boil, then reduce heat, cover, and simmer for about 1 hour, stirring occasionally, until meat is cooked and sauce is well reduced.

Cook pasta in a large saucepan of lightly salted boiling water for 10-12 minutes, or until just cooked or al dente. Drain thoroughly and divide between warmed serving plates. Spoon the meat sauce over the pasta, sprinkle with Parmesan cheese and serve with hot garlic bread.

Serves 4-6

COOK'S TIP: To thicken meat sauce, uncover pan and increase heat slightly 15-20 minutes before the end of cooking time.

— HAM & GORGONZOLA SAUCE —

2 tablespoons olive oil
1 leek, washed and sliced
8oz button mushrooms, sliced
1 clove garlic, crushed
2 tablespoons dry sherry
5fl oz heavy cream
salt and freshly ground black pepper
4oz lean smoked ham, diced
4oz Gorgonzola cheese, diced
2 tablespoons chopped fresh parsley
1lb 2oz fresh tagliatelle
herb sprigs, to garnish

Heat oil in a skillet, add leek, mushrooms, and garlic, and sauté for 8-10 minutes.

Add sherry and cook over a fairly high heat, stirring frequently, until most of liquid has evaporated. Reduce heat, stir in cream, and salt and pepper, and cook gently for 1-2 minutes. Stir in ham, cheese, and chopped parsley, and heat gently until hot, stirring.

Meanwhile, cook pasta in a large saucepan of lightly salted boiling water for 3 minutes, or until just cooked or al dente. Drain thoroughly and return to rinsed-out pan. Add ham and cheese sauce to pasta, and toss well to mix. Serve on warmed plates and garnish with herb sprigs. Serve with a green salad.

Serves 4

VARIATION: Use lean smoked chicken or turkey in place of ham.

– FRAZZLED PROSCIUTTO SAUCE –

2 tablespoons olive oil
12 thin slices of prosciutto, about 6oz
4 shallots, finely chopped
2 zucchini, finely chopped
1 tablespoon chopped fresh flat-leaf parsley
1 tablespoon chopped fresh basil
1 tablespoon chopped fresh oregano or marjoram
10oz crème fraîche
salt and freshly ground black pepper
1lb 2oz fresh fusilli
herb sprigs, to garnish

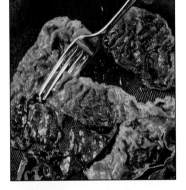

Heat 1 tablespoon oil in a non-stick skillet, cook prosciutto over a fairly high heat, turning frequently, until crinkled and crisp.

Transfer to a plate, set aside, and keep hot. Add remaining oil to skillet and heat until hot, then add shallots and cook for 3 minutes, stirring occasionally. Add zucchini and cook for a further 7 minutes, stirring frequently, until vegetables are just cooked. Stir in chopped herbs, crème fraîche, and salt and pepper, and heat gently until hot, stirring.

Meanwhile, cook pasta in a large saucepan of lightly salted boiling water for 3 minutes, or until just cooked or al dente. Drain thoroughly and return to rinsed-out pan. Snip frazzled prosciutto into thin strips or pieces and stir into herb sauce. Pour sauce over pasta and toss well to mix. Serve on warmed plates and garnish with herb sprigs. Serve with a mixed leaf salad.

Serves 4

— SWEET & SOUR PORK SAUCE —

12oz dried fettuccine
salt and freshly ground black pepper
2 tablespoons sunflower oil
2 zucchini, thinly sliced
1 red bell pepper, seeded and sliced
1 bunch scallions, chopped
1 clove garlic, crushed
1lb lean pork fillet, cut into thin strips
1 tablespoon cornstarch
scant ½ cup apple juice
scant ½ cup vegetable stock
2 tablespoons light soy sauce
2 tablespoons dry sherry
2 tablespoons red wine vinegar
2 tablespoons honey
2 tablespoons tomato catsup

Cook pasta in a large saucepan of lightly salted boiling water for 10-12 minutes, or until just cooked or al dente. Meanwhile, heat oil in a wok or large skillet, add zucchini, bell pepper, scallions, and garlic, and stir-fry over a fairly high heat for 3 minutes. Add pork and stir-fry for about 5 minutes, or until cooked.

Blend cornstarch with apple juice and add to the wok together with stock, soy sauce, sherry, vinegar, honey, tomato catsup, and salt and pepper. Stir-fry until sauce comes to a boil and thickens, then simmer for 2-3 minutes, stirring frequently. Drain pasta and serve on warmed plates. Spoon pork sauce over pasta and serve.

Serves 4

VARIATION: Use lean beef or chicken breast in place of pork.

— HERBY SAUSAGE & GARLIC —

2 tablespoons butter
1 tablespoon olive oil
1 red onion, finely chopped
2 cloves garlic, finely chopped
1 x 14oz can AND 1 x 8oz can chopped tomatoes
scant ½ cup red wine
salt and freshly ground black pepper
12 thin herby sausages, about 12oz
12oz dried wholewheat fusilli pasta
1 tablespoon chopped fresh parsley
1 tablespoon chopped fresh oregano
1-2oz freshly shaved Parmesan, to garnish

Heat butter and oil in a saucepan until butter has melted. Add onion and garlic, and cook gently for 5 minutes, stirring occasionally. Stir in tomatoes, wine, and salt and pepper, and bring to a boil. Cook, uncovered, over a moderate heat for 20-25 minutes, stirring occasionally, until sauce is thick and pulpy. Meanwhile, preheat broiler to high. Broil sausages for about 15 minutes, turning occasionally, until thoroughly cooked, and brown and crisp on the outside. Cut sausages into slices.

In the meantime, cook pasta in a large saucepan of lightly salted boiling water for 10 minutes, or until just cooked or al dente. Drain thoroughly and return to rinsed-out pan. Add sausage slices and chopped herbs to tomato sauce and stir well. Pour over pasta and toss well to mix. Serve on warmed plates and sprinkle with shavings of Parmesan cheese to garnish. Serve with warm ciabatta bread.

Serves 4-6

— BRANDIED CHICKEN LIVERS —

2 tablespoons butter
1 tablespoon sunflower oil
4 shallots, thinly sliced
1 clove garlic, crushed
14oz chicken livers, chopped
6oz mushrooms, sliced
scant ½ cup brandy
4 tablespoons crème fraîche
1 tablespoon chopped fresh parsley
1 tablespoon chopped fresh marjoram or oregano
salt and freshly ground black pepper
1lb 2oz fresh garlic and herb tagliatelle
herb sprigs, to garnish

Heat butter and oil in a large skillet until butter has melted.

Add shallots and garlic, and cook for 5 minutes, stirring occasionally. Add chicken livers and mushrooms, and cook over a fairly high heat, stirring frequently, until chicken livers are sealed and browned all over. Stir in brandy and cook over a high heat for 3-5 minutes, stirring frequently, until liquid has reduced by about half. Reduce heat, stir in the crème fraîche, chopped herbs, and salt and pepper, and heat gently until hot.

Meanwhile, cook pasta in a large saucepan of lightly salted boiling water for 3 minutes, or until just cooked or al dente. Drain thoroughly. Serve pasta on warmed plates and spoon sauce over the top. Garnish with herb sprigs and serve with a mixed baby leaf salad.

Serves 4

VARIATION: Use sliced zucchini in place of mushrooms.

— SMOKED TROUT & ALMONDS —

2 tablespoons sunflower oil
2 leeks, washed and thinly sliced
2 zucchini, thinly sliced
2 tablespoons butter
¼ cup all-purpose flour
2 cups fish or vegetable stock
⅔ cup dry white wine
8oz skinless smoked trout fillets, chopped
2-3 teaspoons chopped fresh tarragon
salt and freshly ground black pepper
1lb 2oz fresh spaghetti
½ cup toasted sliced almonds

Heat oil in a skillet, add leeks and zucchini, and cook gently for 8-10 minutes, stirring occasionally, until softened.

Meanwhile, melt butter in a saucepan, add flour, and cook gently for 1 minute, stirring. Gradually whisk in stock and wine, then heat gently, whisking continuously, until sauce is thickened and smooth. Simmer gently for 2 minutes, stirring.

Stir leek mixture, smoked trout, tarragon, and salt and pepper into sauce and heat gently, stirring occasionally, until very hot. In the meantime, cook pasta in a large saucepan of lightly salted boiling water for 3 minutes, or until just cooked or al dente. Drain thoroughly and return to the rinsed-out pan. Add trout sauce and almonds to pasta, and toss well to mix. Serve with soft bread rolls.

Serves 4-6

— TUNA & PEPPERCORN SAUCE —

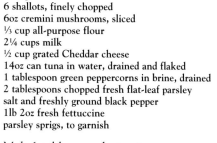

¼ cup butter
6 shallots, finely chopped
6oz cremini mushrooms, sliced
⅓ cup all-purpose flour
2¼ cups milk
½ cup grated Cheddar cheese
14oz can tuna in water, drained and flaked
1 tablespoon green peppercorns in brine, drained
2 tablespoons chopped fresh flat-leaf parsley
salt and freshly ground black pepper
1lb 2oz fresh fettuccine
parsley sprigs, to garnish

Melt 1 tablespoon butter in a saucepan, add shallots and mushrooms, and sauté gently for about 10 minutes, until softened.

Meanwhile, put remaining butter in a separate saucepan with flour and milk. Heat gently, whisking continuously, until sauce is thickened and smooth. Simmer gently for 3 minutes, stirring. Remove pan from heat and stir in cheese until melted, then stir in shallots, mushrooms, tuna, peppercorns, chopped parsley, and salt and pepper. Heat gently until hot, stirring occasionally.

In the meantime, cook pasta in a large saucepan of lightly salted boiling water for 3 minutes, or until just cooked or al dente. Drain thoroughly and return to the rinsed-out saucepan. Add fish sauce to pasta and toss well to mix. Serve on warmed plates and garnish with parsley sprigs. Serve with fresh crusty bread.

Serves 4

VARIATION: Use canned salmon in place of tuna.

SPICY SHRIMP & TOMATO SAUCE

6oz small broccoli flowerets
3 tablespoons butter
1 leek, washed and sliced
2 cloves garlic, crushed
1½ teaspoons hot chili powder
1 teaspoon ground coriander
1 teaspoon ground cumin
6oz button mushrooms, sliced
⅔ cup dry white wine
14oz can chopped tomatoes
salt and freshly ground black pepper
12oz cooked, peeled jumbo shrimp
12oz dried penne
2 tablespoons chopped fresh cilantro

Cook broccoli in a saucepan of boiling water for 5 minutes, or until just tender. Drain well and set aside. Melt butter in a large saucepan, add leek and garlic, and cook gently for 5 minutes, stirring occasionally. Add ground spices and cook for 1 minute, stirring. Add mushrooms, wine, tomatoes, and salt and pepper, and stir to mix. Bring to a boil, then reduce heat, cover and simmer for 10 minutes, stirring occasionally. Uncover pan, increase heat, and cook for a further 10 minutes, stirring occasionally, until sauce has thickened slightly.

Stir in broccoli and shrimp, and cook for 5 minutes or until very hot. Meanwhile, cook pasta in a large saucepan of lightly salted boiling water for 10 minutes, or until just cooked or al dente. Drain thoroughly and serve on warmed plates. Stir chopped cilantro into tomato sauce, then spoon sauce over pasta. Serve with crusty fresh bread.

Serves 4

——CLAM & CORN CAPELLINI——

2¼lb fresh clams in their shells, cleaned
4 tablespoons dry white wine
1 tablespoon butter
1 tablespoon olive oil
2 leeks, washed and sliced
1 clove garlic, crushed
7oz can corn, drained
8oz frozen petit pois, thawed
10fl oz heavy cream
salt and freshly ground black pepper
2 tablespoons chopped fresh flat-leaf parsley
1lb 2oz fresh capellini

Put clams in a large saucepan with wine. Cover and cook for 5-7 minutes, shaking pan occasionally, until clams have opened.

Strain clams, reserving 6 tablespoons of cooking liquid. Discard any clams whose shells have not opened. Remove most of clams from their shells, but reserve a few in shells for garnish. Set aside and keep hot. Heat butter and oil in a saucepan until butter is melted, then add leeks and garlic, and cook gently for 10 minutes, stirring occasionally, until softened. Add corn, petit pois, cream, reserved clam liquid, and salt and pepper, and cook gently for 3-4 minutes, stirring occasionally, until hot. Stir in chopped parsley and shelled clams.

Meanwhile, cook pasta in a large saucepan of lightly salted boiling water for 3 minutes, or until just cooked or al dente. Drain thoroughly, then serve on warmed plates. Spoon clam sauce over pasta, and serve garnished with clams in their shells, and parsley sprigs if you like. Serve with a mixed green salad.

Serves 4

—STILTON & WALNUT SAUCE—

12oz dried farfalle or spirali
salt and freshly ground black pepper
1 tablespoon olive oil
4 shallots, finely chopped
1 clove garlic, crushed
7oz crème fraîche
2 tablespoons chopped fresh chives
1 cup walnut pieces
4oz Stilton cheese, crumbled
herb sprigs, to garnish

Cook pasta in a large saucepan of lightly salted boiling water for 10 minutes, or until just cooked or al dente.

Meanwhile, heat oil in a saucepan, add shallots and garlic, and cook gently for 8-10 minutes, stirring occasionally, until softened. Stir in crème fraîche and heat gently until bubbling. Stir in chopped chives, and salt and pepper.

Drain pasta thoroughly and return to rinsed-out pan. Add cream sauce, walnuts, and Stilton and toss well to mix. Serve on warmed plates, and garnish with herb sprigs. Serve with warm, crusty bread rolls.

Serves 4

VARIATION: Use other blue cheese such as Gorgonzola, Dolcelatte or Cambozola (blue Brie) in place of Stilton.

— CHUNKY TOMATO & BASIL —

1 tablespoon olive oil
6 shallots, finely chopped
2 cloves garlic, finely chopped
2 sticks celery, finely chopped
1½lb ripe plum tomatoes, skinned, seeded
   and roughly chopped
4 sun-dried tomatoes in oil, drained and chopped
⅔ cup red wine
1 tablespoon tomato paste
salt and freshly ground black pepper
12oz dried orecchiette
3-4 tablespoons chopped fresh basil

Heat oil in a large saucepan, add shallots, garlic, and celery, and cook gently for 5 minutes, stirring occasionally.

Add tomatoes, sun-dried tomatoes, wine, tomato paste, and salt and pepper, and mix well. Bring to a boil, then reduce heat, cover and simmer for 10 minutes, stirring occasionally. Uncover pan, increase heat slightly and cook for a further 10-15 minutes, stirring frequently, until sauce has thickened slightly.

Meanwhile, cook pasta in a large saucepan of lightly salted boiling water for 12-15 minutes, or until just cooked or al dente. Drain thoroughly and return to rinsed-out pan. Add tomato sauce and chopped basil and toss well to mix. Serve on warmed plates, and garnish with basil sprigs if you like. Serve with hot cheese-topped garlic bread.

Serves 4

– GARLIC & CHILI TAGLIATELLE –

12oz dried tricolor tagliatelle
salt and freshly ground black pepper
4 tablespoons olive oil
2 shallots, finely chopped
2 small fresh red chilies, seeded and finely chopped
3 cloves garlic, crushed
4 sun-dried tomatoes in oil, drained and chopped
3 tablespoons chopped fresh basil
¾ cup finely grated fresh Parmesan cheese, to serve
basil sprigs, to garnish

Cook pasta in a large saucepan of lightly salted boiling water for 10-12 minutes, or until just cooked or al dente.

Meanwhile, heat 1 tablespoon oil in a large saucepan, add shallots, chilies, and garlic and cook over a moderate heat for about 5 minutes, stirring frequently, until softened. Add remaining oil to pan with sun-dried tomatoes and salt and pepper, and heat gently until hot.

Drain pasta thoroughly and return to rinsed-out pan. Add oil mixture with chopped basil and toss well to mix. Serve on warmed plates and sprinkle generously with Parmesan cheese. Garnish with basil sprigs and serve with crusty French bread.

Serves 4

VARIATION: Use fresh green chilies in place of red chilies.

—ROAST BELL PEPPER & FENNEL—

4 fennel bulbs
4 red bell peppers, seeded and cut into thick slices
5 tablespoons olive oil
juice of 1 lemon
salt and freshly ground black pepper
1lb 2oz fresh strozzapretti
8oz mozzarella cheese, diced
2 tablespoons chopped fresh flat-leaf parsley
flat-leaf parsley sprigs, to garnish

Preheat oven to 400F (200C). Trim fennel bulbs, cutting off fibrous tops. Cut each bulb into quarters and remove and discard core.

Cook fennel in a saucepan of boiling water for 5 minutes. Drain thoroughly. Lightly grease a shallow ovenproof dish or baking pan. Put fennel in the prepared dish with bell peppers. Whisk oil, lemon juice, and salt and pepper together, and drizzle over fennel and bell peppers. Toss gently to mix. Bake in the oven for about 30 minutes, stirring once or twice, until vegetables are tender and tinged brown around edges. Meanwhile, cook pasta in a large saucepan of lightly salted boiling water for 3 minutes, or until just cooked or al dente.

Scatter mozzarella and chopped parsley over vegetables and stir gently to mix. Drain pasta thoroughly and serve on warmed plates. Spoon vegetable mixture and juices over pasta. Alternatively, lightly toss the vegetables, cheese, and pasta together before serving. Garnish with parsley sprigs and serve with warm crusty ciabatta bread.

Serves 4

VARIATION: Use yellow bell peppers in place of red bell peppers.

—— HAZELNUT PESTO SAUCE ——

2oz basil leaves
⅓ cup hazelnuts, lightly toasted
scant ½ cup olive oil
2 cloves garlic, crushed
¾ cup finely grated fresh Parmesan cheese
salt and freshly ground black pepper
12oz dried plain or tomato spaghetti
basil sprigs, to garnish

Put basil leaves, hazelnuts, olive oil, and garlic in a small blender or food processor and blend until smooth and well mixed.

Add Parmesan cheese, and salt and pepper, and blend briefly to mix. Transfer to a small bowl, cover and set aside. Cook pasta in a large saucepan of lightly salted boiling water for 10-12 minutes, or until just cooked or al dente. Drain thoroughly and return to rinsed-out pan.

Add pesto sauce and toss lightly to mix. Serve on warmed plates and garnish with basil sprigs. Serve with a mixed leaf salad.

Serves 4

VARIATIONS: Use lightly toasted pine nuts or almonds in place of hazelnuts. Use 1oz fresh parsley in place of 1oz basil.

PARMESAN & PINE NUTS

12oz dried fusilli lunghi (long fusilli pasta)
salt and freshly ground black pepper
4oz pine nuts
¼ cup butter
1 small onion, finely chopped
2 zucchini, cut into thin strips
6 tablespoons crème fraîche
1 cup finely grated fresh Parmesan cheese
3 tablespoons chopped fresh flat-leaf parsley
herb sprigs, to garnish

Cook pasta in a large saucepan of lightly salted boiling water for 10-12 minutes, or until just cooked or al dente.

Meanwhile, preheat broiler to high. Spread pine nuts out on a baking sheet and place under broiler for 2-3 minutes, stirring occasionally, until lightly toasted all over. Remove from broiler and set aside. Melt butter in a large skillet, add onion and zucchini, and cook for about 8 minutes, stirring occasionally, until tender. Stir in crème fraîche and pine nuts, and heat gently until bubbling. Remove pan from heat, stir in half the Parmesan, the salt and pepper, and mix well.

Drain pasta thoroughly and return to rinsed-out saucepan. Add pine nut sauce and chopped parsley, and toss well to mix. Serve on warmed plates and sprinkle with remaining Parmesan. Garnish with herb sprigs and serve with warm crusty bread.

Serves 4

VARIATION: Use chopped fresh basil or cilantro in place of parsley.

— ASPARAGUS & GOAT CHEESE —

14oz extra fine asparagus, cut in half
¼ cup butter, melted
2 cloves garlic, crushed
⅔ cup heavy cream
3 tablespoons chopped fresh basil
salt and freshly ground black pepper
1lb 2oz fresh tagliatelle
6oz soft goat cheese, crumbled
basil sprigs, to garnish

Steam asparagus over a pan of boiling water for 6-8 minutes or until just tender. Drain well.

Melt butter in a saucepan, add garlic and asparagus, and cook for 1-2 minutes, stirring occasionally. Stir in cream, chopped basil, and salt and pepper, and heat gently until hot, stirring occasionally. Meanwhile, cook pasta in a large saucepan of lightly salted boiling water for 3 minutes, or until just cooked or al dente. Drain thoroughly and return to rinsed-out saucepan.

Add asparagus sauce and goat cheese to pasta and toss lightly to mix. Serve on warmed plates and garnish with basil sprigs. Serve with a mixed baby leaf salad.

Serves 4

VARIATION: Use other cheese such as Brie or feta in place of goat cheese.

CLASSIC LASAGNE

1 tablespoon olive oil
2 onions, chopped
1 clove garlic, crushed
2 carrots, finely chopped
1lb 2oz lean ground beef
6oz mushrooms, chopped
14oz can chopped tomatoes
2 tablespoons tomato paste
scant 1 cup dry white wine
2 teaspoons dried Italian herb seasoning
salt and freshly ground black pepper
⅓ cup butter
9 tablespoons all-purpose flour
3¾ cups milk
2 cups grated Cheddar or pecorino cheese
9 fresh lasagne sheets

Heat oil in a large pan, add onions, garlic, and carrots, and cook for 5 minutes, stirring. Add beef and cook until browned. Stir in mushrooms, tomatoes, tomato paste, wine, herbs, and salt and pepper, and mix well. Bring to a boil, reduce heat, cover, and simmer for 45 minutes, stirring occasionally. Preheat oven to 350F (180C). Lightly grease a large ovenproof dish; set aside. Melt butter in a saucepan, add flour, and cook gently for 1 minute, stirring. Gradually whisk in milk, then heat gently, whisking continuously, until thick and smooth. Simmer for 2 minutes.

Remove pan from heat, whisk in 1¼ cups cheese, then cover sauce with parchment paper; set aside. Part-cook lasagne according to pack directions. Remove from pan, refresh under cold running water, and drain well on paper towels. Spoon one-third of meat sauce into prepared dish, cover with 3 sheets of lasagne, and top with some cheese sauce. Repeat twice, pouring remaining cheese sauce over pasta. Sprinkle with remaining cheese. Bake for 45 minutes or until golden.

Serves 4-6

BEEF & MACARONI PIE

1 tablespoon sunflower oil
1 onion, chopped
1 clove garlic, crushed
1 stick celery, finely chopped
2 small fresh red chilies, seeded and finely chopped
12oz lean ground beef
4oz button mushrooms, chopped
1 red bell pepper, seeded and diced
14oz can chopped tomatoes
⅔ cup dry white wine
salt and freshly ground black pepper
1⅔ cups dried short-cut macaroni
12oz Greek yogurt
2 eggs
½ cup finely grated fresh Parmesan cheese
herb sprigs, to garnish

Heat oil in a large saucepan, add onion, garlic, celery, and chilies, and cook for 5 minutes, stirring occasionally. Add beef and cook until browned all over, stirring. Add mushrooms, red bell pepper, tomatoes, wine, and salt and pepper, and mix well. Bring to a boil, then reduce heat, cover, and simmer for 45 minutes, stirring occasionally. Preheat oven to 375F (190C). Lightly grease an ovenproof dish and set aside. Cook macaroni in a large saucepan of lightly salted boiling water for 8-10 minutes, or until just cooked. Drain thoroughly.

Mix meat sauce and macaroni together and spoon into prepared dish. Lightly whisk yogurt, eggs, and salt and pepper together and pour evenly over macaroni mixture. Sprinkle Parmesan over the top. Bake in the oven for 30 minutes, or until golden brown. Garnish with herb sprigs and serve with a mixed dark leaf salad.

Serves 4-6

VARIATION: Use lean ground lamb or pork in place of beef.

——LAMB & BELL PEPPER BAKE——

1 tablespoon olive oil
2 shallots, finely chopped
1 leek, washed and finely chopped
2 cloves garlic, crushed
1 small green bell pepper, seeded and finely chopped
12oz lean ground lamb
7fl oz passata (sieved tomatoes)
1 tablespoon chopped fresh oregano
1 tablespoon chopped fresh thyme
salt and freshly ground black pepper
12 fresh lasagne sheets
14oz natural whole milk yogurt
2 eggs
¼ cup finely grated Gruyère cheese
herb sprigs, to garnish

Heat oil in a saucepan, add shallots, leek, garlic, and green bell pepper, and cook for 5 minutes, stirring occasionally. Add lamb and cook until browned all over, stirring frequently. Stir in passata, chopped herbs, and salt and pepper, and mix well. Bring to a boil, then reduce heat, cover, and simmer for 20 minutes, stirring occasionally. Uncover, increase the heat slightly, and cook for a further 8-10 minutes, stirring frequently, until most of liquid has evaporated. Preheat the oven to 400F (200C). Lightly butter a shallow ovenproof dish and set aside.

Cook lasagne in a large pan of lightly salted boiling water for 2 minutes, drain, refresh under cold running water; drain again. Lay lasagne out on counter and spoon some lamb mixture along long edge of each sheet. Roll lasagne to make cannelloni. Arrange cannelloni, seam-side down, in prepared dish. Lightly beat yogurt, eggs, and salt and pepper together and pour over cannelloni. Sprinkle cheese over top. Bake for 25-30 minutes, or until golden. Garnish with herb sprigs.

Serves 4-6

— TAGLIATELLE CARBONARA —

12oz dried tagliatelle
salt and freshly ground black pepper
¼ cup butter
1 tablespoon olive oil
1 onion, finely chopped
8oz smoked bacon slices, chopped
3 eggs, beaten
6 tablespoons heavy cream
½ cup finely grated pecorino cheese
¾ cup finely grated fresh Parmesan cheese
chopped fresh chives, to garnish

Cook pasta in a large saucepan of lightly salted boiling water for 10-12 minutes, or until just cooked or al dente.

Meanwhile, heat butter and oil in a saucepan until butter is melted. Add onion and cook for 5 minutes, stirring occasionally, until softened. Add bacon and cook for 5 minutes, stirring frequently, until bacon is cooked. Remove pan from the heat and set aside. Mix eggs, cream, pecorino cheese, ½ cup Parmesan, and salt and pepper together in a bowl. Drain pasta thoroughly and return to a clean pan. Add bacon mixture and toss to mix.

Add egg mixture and cook gently, tossing continuously until eggs are just cooked. Serve, sprinkled with remaining Parmesan. Garnish with chopped fresh chives and serve with fresh crusty bread.

Serves 4

VARIATIONS: Use Cheddar cheese in place of pecorino. Use spaghetti or bucatini in place of tagliatelle.

—— FENNEL & BACON GRATIN ——

3 fennel bulbs, trimmed
salt and freshly ground black pepper
¼ cup butter
8oz dried penne
8oz rindless smoked bacon slices, chopped
4 tablespoons all-purpose flour
2 cups milk
⅔ cup heavy cream
1 cup grated Cheddar cheese
3 tablespoons fresh bread crumbs
herb sprigs, to garnish

Cut fennel lengthways into ¼in slices. Cook in a pan of lightly salted boiling water for 10-15 minutes or until tender.

Remove from pan using a slotted spoon. Set pan and cooking water aside. Put fennel in a bowl, add 3 teaspoons butter and toss to mix. Set aside and keep warm. Cook pasta in reserved pan of boiling cooking water for 10 minutes, or until just cooked or al dente. Melt 3 teaspoons of remaining butter in a pan, add bacon, and cook over a fairly high heat for 5 minutes, stirring, until cooked. Remove bacon from pan using a slotted spoon and add to fennel. Set aside and keep hot. Add remaining butter to juices in pan; heat, add flour and cook for 1 minute, stirring.

Gradually whisk in milk and cream, heat gently, whisking, until sauce is thickened. Simmer for 2 minutes, stirring. Remove pan from heat and whisk in ¾ cup cheese and salt and pepper. Drain pasta thoroughly and toss with fennel and bacon. Pour cheese sauce over pasta and toss to mix. Transfer to a flameproof dish. Preheat broiler to high. Mix remaining cheese and bread crumbs and sprinkle over the top. Broil for a few minutes until golden. Garnish with herb sprigs.

Serves 4

— PEA, HAM, & PARSLEY BAKE —

8oz dried rigatoni
salt and freshly ground black pepper
3 tablespoons butter
⅓ cup all-purpose flour
3¼ cups milk
8oz lean smoked ham, diced
8oz frozen peas
4 tablespoons chopped fresh parsley
½ cup grated Cheddar cheese (optional)
flat-leaf parsley sprigs, to garnish

Preheat the oven to 400F (200C). Lightly butter an ovenproof dish; set aside.

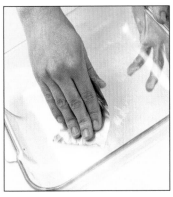

Cook pasta in a large saucepan of lightly salted boiling water for about 10 minutes, or until just cooked or al dente. Drain well, set aside, and keep warm. Meanwhile, put butter, flour, and milk in a separate saucepan. Heat gently, whisking continuously, until sauce is thickened and smooth. Simmer gently for 3 minutes, stirring. Remove pan from the heat, add pasta, ham, peas, chopped parsley, and salt and pepper, and stir gently to mix.

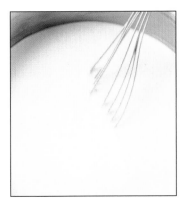

Transfer to prepared dish and sprinkle with Cheddar cheese, if using. Bake in the oven for 20-25 minutes, or until lightly browned and bubbling. Garnish with parsley sprigs and serve with cooked vegetables such as green beans and broiled tomatoes.

Serves 4

VARIATIONS: Use cooked smoked chicken or turkey in place of ham. Use fresh Parmesan cheese in place of Cheddar.

— PANCETTA & CHILI PENNE —

1½lb plum tomatoes
3 tablespoons butter
6 shallots, finely chopped
1 large clove garlic, crushed
2 fresh red chilies, seeded and finely chopped
2 sticks celery, finely chopped
8oz pancetta, diced
6oz mushrooms, finely chopped
⅔ cup red wine
4 sun-dried tomatoes in oil, drained and chopped
salt and freshly ground black pepper
1lb 2oz fresh penne rigate
2 tablespoons chopped fresh oregano
oregano sprigs, to garnish

Put plum tomatoes in a large bowl and cover with boiling water. Leave for 30-60 seconds, then drain and peel; deseed and chop them. Set aside. Melt butter in a saucepan, add shallots, garlic, chilies, celery, and pancetta, and cook for 5 minutes, stirring. Add chopped plum tomatoes, mushrooms, wine, sun-dried tomatoes,, and salt and pepper, and stir to mix. Bring to a boil, then cover and simmer for 10 minutes, stirring occasionally. Uncover pan, increase heat slightly and cook for 10-15 minutes, stirring occasionally, until sauce has thickened slightly.

Meanwhile, cook pasta in a large saucepan of lightly salted boiling water for 3-5 minutes, or until just cooked or al dente. Drain thoroughly and return to the rinsed-out pan. Add tomato sauce and chopped oregano, and toss well to mix. Garnish with oregano sprigs, and serve with a mixed leaf salad and hot crusty garlic bread.

Serves 4

VARIATION: Use chorizo in place of pancetta.

— SPICED PORK SPAGHETTINI —

1 tablespoon sunflower oil
2 red onions, chopped
1 large red bell pepper, seeded and diced
12oz lean ground pork
1 tablespoon all-purpose flour
2 teaspoons ground cumin
1½ teaspoons hot chilli powder
1 teaspoon ground coriander
14oz can chopped tomatoes
2 tablespoons tomato paste
1¼ cups pork or vegetable stock
salt and freshly ground black pepper
8oz cremini mushrooms, sliced
1lb 2oz fresh spaghettini
herb sprigs, to garnish

Heat oil in a large saucepan, add onions and red bell pepper, and cook gently for 5 minutes, stirring occasionally. Add ground pork and cook until browned all over, stirring frequently. Add flour and ground spices, and cook for 1 minute, stirring. Stir in tomatoes, tomato paste, stock, and salt and pepper, and mix well. Bring to a boil, then reduce the heat, cover and simmer for 30 minutes, stirring occasionally.

Stir in mushrooms, cover and simmer for a further 30 minutes, stirring occasionally. Meanwhile, cook pasta in a large pan of lightly salted boiling water for 3 minutes, or until just cooked or al dente. Drain thoroughly and serve on warmed plates. Spoon sauce over pasta and garnish with herb sprigs. Serve with warm crusty bread.

Serves 4-6

VARIATION: Use lean ground lamb or turkey in place of pork.

TORTELLONI GRATIN

8oz small broccoli flowerets
1lb fresh ham and cheese tortelloni
salt and freshly ground black pepper
⅓ cup butter
4 shallots, finely chopped
4oz button mushrooms, sliced
½ cup all-purpose flour
2½ cups milk
⅔ cup heavy cream
1 cup grated pecorino cheese
3 tablespoons fresh bread crumbs
herb sprigs, to garnish

Cook broccoli in a large saucepan of boiling water for 5 minutes, or until tender. Drain well, set aside, and keep warm.

Using the same pan, cook pasta in lightly salted boiling water for 4-5 minutes, or until just cooked or al dente. Drain well, add to broccoli, and keep warm. Melt 2 tablespoons butter in a saucepan and sauté shallots and mushrooms for 5-6 minutes, or until softened. Remove from pan using a slotted spoon and add to pasta. Stir gently to mix. Add remaining butter to pan and heat until melted. Add flour and cook gently for 1 minute, stirring. Gradually whisk in milk and cream, then cook, whisking, until sauce is thickened. Simmer gently for 2 minutes, stirring.

Remove pan from the heat and whisk in ¼ cup pecorino cheese. Pour cheese sauce over pasta and vegetables, and toss well to mix. Preheat broiler to high. Transfer pasta mixture to a flameproof dish. Mix together remaining cheese and bread crumbs, and sprinkle over the top. Place under broiler for 2-3 minutes or until golden and bubbling. Garnish with herb sprigs and serve with cooked vegetables such as baby carrots and zucchini.

Serves 4-6

TOMATO & CHORIZO TORTELLINI

2 tablespoons olive oil
1 red onion, finely chopped
1 red bell pepper, seeded and diced
2 carrots, finely chopped
2 cloves garlic, crushed
6oz chorizo, thinly sliced
14oz can chopped tomatoes
4 tablespoons dry white wine
2 tablespoons sun-dried tomato paste
salt and freshly ground black pepper
14oz dried tortellini, such as cheese
    and ham tortellini
3 tablespoons chopped fresh basil
fresh Parmesan cheese shavings, to garnish

Heat oil in a saucepan, add onion, red bell pepper, carrots, and garlic and cook for 5 minutes, stirring occasionally. Add chorizo and cook for 1 minute, stirring. Add tomatoes, wine, tomato paste, and salt and pepper and mix well. Bring to a boil, then reduce heat, cover and simmer for 15 minutes, stirring occasionally. Uncover, increase heat slightly, and cook for a further 10-15 minutes, stirring occasionally, until sauce is cooked and has thickened slightly.

Meanwhile, cook pasta in a large saucepan of lightly salted boiling water for 10 minutes, or until cooked and tender. Drain pasta thoroughly and return it to the rinsed-out pan. Add chorizo sauce and chopped basil, and toss well to mix. Serve on warmed plates and garnish with shavings of Parmesan cheese. Serve with hot crusty garlic and herb bread.

Serves 4

-TURKEY & BROCCOLI LASAGNE-

10oz small broccoli flowerets
1 tablespoon sunflower oil
1 onion, chopped
1 clove garlic, crushed
2 sticks celery, finely chopped
8oz mushrooms, sliced
2 zucchini, sliced
3 tablespoons butter
⅓ cup all-purpose flour
3¾ cups milk
1½ cups grated Cheddar cheese
salt and freshly ground black pepper
14oz cooked skinless, boneless turkey
  breast, diced
8 sheets no pre-cook lasagne verdi
herb sprigs, to garnish

Preheat the oven to 350F (180C). Lightly grease a shallow ovenproof dish and set aside. Cook broccoli in a saucepan of boiling water for 2 minutes. Drain well and set aside. Heat oil in a large saucepan, add onion, garlic, celery, mushrooms, and zucchini, and cook for 5 minutes, stirring occasionally. Meanwhile, melt butter in a separate saucepan, add flour and cook gently for 1 minute, stirring. Gradually whisk in milk, then heat gently, whisking, until the sauce is thickened and smooth. Simmer gently for 2 minutes, stirring.

Remove the pan from heat and stir in 1¼ cups cheese and salt and pepper. Set aside about 1¼ cups cheese sauce. Mix remaining sauce with vegetables, broccoli, and turkey. Spoon half turkey mixture into prepared dish and cover with half the lasagne. Repeat these layers, then pour reserved cheese sauce over lasagne, to cover. Sprinkle with remaining cheese. Bake for 45 minutes, or until cooked and golden. Garnish with herb sprigs and serve with a mixed green salad.

Serves 4-6

— CAJUN CHICKEN FETTUCCINE —

1 tablespoon sunflower oil
6 shallots, thinly sliced
1 green bell pepper, seeded and sliced
2 carrots, cut into matchstick strips
8oz button mushrooms, halved
1lb skinless, boneless chicken breast,
  cut into thin strips
1 tablespoon Cajun seasoning
1 tablespoon cornstarch
2 tablespoons dry sherry
1¼ cups chicken stock
2 tablespoons tomato paste
salt and freshly ground black pepper
1lb 2oz fresh fettuccine
chopped fresh parsley, to garnish

Heat oil in a wok or large skillet, add shallots, green bell pepper, carrots, and mushrooms, and stir-fry for 3 minutes. Add chicken and stir-fry for a further 3-4 minutes, or until cooked; then add Cajun seasoning and stir-fry for 1 minute. Blend cornstarch with sherry and add to the wok with stock, tomato paste, and salt and pepper. Stir-fry until hot and bubbling, then simmer gently for 2-3 minutes.

Meanwhile, cook pasta in a large saucepan of lightly salted boiling water for 3 minutes, or until just cooked or al dente. Drain thoroughly and serve on warmed plates. Spoon chicken sauce over pasta and sprinkle with chopped parsley to garnish. Serve with warm crusty bread.

Serves 4

VARIATIONS: Use turkey breast or lean pork or beef in place of chicken. Use Chinese 5-spice seasoning in place of Cajun seasoning.

CHICKEN CANNELLONI

8oz cooked skinless, boneless chicken
  breast, finely chopped
½ cup full-fat soft cheese
½ cup pine nuts, toasted and finely chopped
⅓ cup sultanas
4 scallions, finely chopped
2 eggs, beaten
2 tablespoons chopped fresh cilantro
salt and freshly ground black pepper
16 dried cannelloni tubes
3 tablespoons butter
⅓ cup all-purpose flour
2½ cups milk
½ cup finely grated fresh Parmesan cheese
cilantro sprigs, to garnish

Preheat the oven to 350F (180C). Lightly
grease a shallow ovenproof dish and set
aside. Put chicken, soft cheese, pine nuts,
sultanas, scallions, eggs, chopped cilantro,
and salt and pepper in a bowl and mix well.
Set aside. Part-cook cannelloni tubes
according to package directions. Remove
from pan, refresh under cold running water,
then drain well on paper towels. Fill each
cannelloni tube with chicken mixture.
Arrange filled tubes in a single layer in
prepared dish. Set aside.

Put butter, flour, and milk in a saucepan and
heat gently, whisking continuously, until
sauce is thickened and smooth. Simmer for
3 minutes, stirring. Pour sauce over filled
cannelloni tubes and sprinkle cheese over
the top. Bake for 35-40 minutes, or until
golden brown. Garnish with cilantro sprigs
and serve with a mixed green salad.

Serves 4

VARIATION: Use cooked smoked or
unsmoked turkey breast in place of chicken.

- SMOKED CHICKEN & LEEK BAKE -

8oz dried tricolour trompretti or fusilli
salt and freshly ground black pepper
⅓ cup butter
3 leeks, washed and sliced
8oz mushrooms, sliced.
1 yellow bell pepper, seeded and sliced
½ cup all-purpose flour
2 cups chicken stock
2 cups milk
1¼ cups grated Cheddar cheese
8oz cooked skinless, boneless smoked
  chicken, diced
3 tablespoons chopped fresh parsley
parsley sprigs, to garnish

Preheat oven to 400F (200C). Lightly grease
an ovenproof dish and set aside. Cook pasta
in a large saucepan of lightly salted boiling
water for 10 minutes, or until just cooked or
al dente. Meanwhile, melt 2 tablespoons
butter in a large skillet, add leeks, mushrooms,
and yellow bell pepper, and cook over a fairly
high heat for 5 minutes, stirring occasionally,
until softened. Remove pan from heat and set
aside. Put remaining butter, flour, stock, and
milk in a saucepan, and heat gently, whisking,
until sauce is thickened. Simmer gently for
3 minutes, stirring.

Remove pan from heat and stir in 1 cup
cheese, chicken, chopped parsley, and salt
and pepper. Drain pasta thoroughly and add
to chicken sauce with leeks, mushrooms,
and yellow bell pepper, and mix well.
Transfer to prepared dish and sprinkle with
remaining cheese. Bake for 25-30 minutes,
or until golden brown and bubbling.
Garnish with parsley sprigs and serve with
crusty bread and a mixed baby leaf salad.

Serves 4

— CHICKEN & ZUCCHINI PASTA —

¼ cup butter
6 shallots, thinly sliced
3 zucchini, cut into matchstick strips
scant ½ cup dry white wine
12oz dried fusilli lunghi (long fusilli pasta)
salt and freshly ground black pepper
12oz cooked skinless, boneless chicken
  breast, cut into thin strips
1 tablespoon chopped fresh tarragon
10oz crème fraîche
¾ cup finely grated fresh Parmesan cheese
tarragon sprigs, to garnish

Melt butter in a saucepan, add shallots and zucchini, and cook gently for 10 minutes, stirring occasionally, until softened.

Add wine and cook over a moderate heat until reduced by half. Meanwhile, cook pasta in a large pan of lightly salted boiling water for 10-12 minutes, or until just cooked or al dente. Add chicken, chopped tarragon, and salt and pepper to shallot mixture, reduce heat, and cook for 2 minutes, stirring.

Stir in crème fraîche and heat gently until hot and bubbling. Stir in Parmesan. Drain pasta thoroughly and return to the rinsed-out pan. Add chicken sauce and toss well to mix. Serve on warmed plates and garnish with tarragon sprigs. Serve with additional Parmesan and warm crusty bread.

Serves 4

VARIATIONS: Use cooked turkey breast or cooked flaked salmon in place of chicken. Use 1 large onion in place of shallots.

— BROILED SCALLOP CAPELLINI —

1½oz basil leaves
½oz fresh flat-leaf parsley
¼ cup pine nuts
2 cloves garlic, crushed
2oz sun-dried tomatoes in oil
  (drained weight)
1 tablespoon tomato paste
8 tablespoons olive oil
½ cup finely grated fresh Parmesan cheese
salt and freshly ground black pepper
1lb shelled medium scallops
1lb 2oz fresh capellini
basil sprigs, to garnish

Put first 6 ingredients in a small blender or food processor with 6 tablespoons oil and blend well. Add Parmesan and salt and pepper, and blend briefly. Set aside. Preheat broiler to high. Thread scallops on to wooden skewers (soak skewers in water beforehand to prevent scorching). Brush with remaining oil and season with salt and plenty of black pepper. Broil for 10 minutes, until cooked and just firm, turning once. Remove scallops from skewers and cut them in half or quarters. Set aside and keep hot.

Meanwhile, cook pasta in a large saucepan of lightly salted boiling water for 3 minutes, or until just cooked or al dente. In the meantime, gently heat the pesto (basil sauce) in a saucepan until hot, stirring occasionally. Drain pasta thoroughly, then return to the rinsed-out pan. Add pesto and toss well to mix, then add scallops and toss gently. Serve on warmed plates and garnish with basil sprigs. Serve with crusty French bread.

Serves 4

— SMOKED HADDOCK LASAGNE —

1lb 2oz skinless smoked haddock fillet
2 bay leaves
3¾ cups milk
1 tablespoon sunflower oil
1 onion, chopped
2 sticks celery, finely chopped
2 zucchini, sliced
6oz mushrooms, sliced
3 tablespoons butter
⅓ cup all-purpose flour
1½ cups grated Cheddar cheese
9 fresh lasagne sheets
8oz frozen peas
3 tablespoons chopped fresh parsley
salt and freshly ground black pepper
3 tablespoons fresh bread crumbs

Preheat oven to 375F (190C). Put fish in a pan with bay leaves and milk. Cover, bring to a boil, then simmer for 6-8 minutes. Heat oil in a saucepan, add onion and celery, and cook for 5 minutes, stirring. Add zucchini and mushrooms, and cook for 5 minutes; set aside. Remove fish from milk using a slotted spoon; flake fish. Discard bay leaves; reserve milk. Melt butter in a saucepan, stir in flour and cook gently for 1 minute. Whisk in reserved milk, then cook, whisking, until thickened. Simmer for 2 minutes. Whisk in 1¼ cups cheese; cover and set aside.

Part-cook lasagne according to package directions. Refresh under cold running water, then drain on paper towels. Drain off liquid from onion mixture. Reserve about 1¼ cups cheese sauce and mix remaining sauce with fish, cooked vegetables, peas, parsley, and salt and pepper. Spoon one-third of fish sauce into ovenproof dish; cover with 3 lasagne sheets. Repeat twice more; pour reserved cheese sauce over. Mix remaining cheese with bread crumbs; sprinkle over top. Bake for 30-40 minutes.

Serves 4

– CREAMY SALMON FETTUCCINE –

2 tablespoons butter
8oz button mushrooms, halved
⅔ cup dry white wine
10oz crème fraîche
10oz smoked salmon, cut into thin strips
   or small chunks
1 tablespoon chopped fresh dill
1 tablespoon creamed horseradish
salt and freshly ground black pepper
1lb 2oz fresh fettuccine
dill sprigs, to garnish

Melt butter in a saucepan, add mushrooms and cook over a moderate heat for 5 minutes, stirring occasionally.

Add wine, bring to a boil and cook over a high heat until reduced by half. Reduce the heat, stir in crème fraîche and bring gently to a boil. Stir in salmon, chopped dill, horseradish, and salt and pepper, and heat gently for a minute or two. Meanwhile, cook pasta in a large saucepan of lightly salted boiling water for 3 minutes, or until just cooked or al dente.

Drain pasta thoroughly and return to the rinsed-out pan. Add salmon sauce and toss well to mix. Serve on warmed plates and garnish with dill sprigs. Serve with cooked fresh vegetables such as broccoli flowerets and baby carrots.

Serves 4

VARIATIONS: Use sliced zucchini in place of mushrooms. Use heavy cream in place of crème fraîche.

—— PESTO COD CANNELLONI ——

12oz skinless cod fillet
2 bay leaves
2 shallots, cut into quarters
1¼ cups milk
2 tablespoons butter
3oz mushrooms, finely chopped
1 small zucchini, finely chopped
4 tablespoons pesto
salt and freshly ground black pepper
12 cannelloni tubes
2 tablespoons all-purpose flour
1 cup grated Cheddar or pecorino cheese
3 tablespoons fresh bread crumbs
basil sprigs, to garnish

Preheat oven to 375F (190C). Put fish in a saucepan with bay leaves, shallots, and milk. Cover, bring gently to a boil, then simmer for 6-8 minutes or until fish flakes. Meanwhile, melt 3 teaspoons butter in a saucepan, add mushrooms and zucchini, and sauté for 5 minutes. Remove pan from heat. Remove fish from milk using a slotted spoon and flake. Remove and discard bay leaves and shallots, and reserve milk. Add fish to mushroom mixture, together with pesto and salt and pepper; mix well. Set aside. Part-cook cannelloni according to package directions.

Refresh cannelloni under cold running water; drain well. Fill with fish mixture and arrange in a single layer in a shallow ovenproof dish. Set aside. Put milk in a saucepan with remaining butter and flour. Heat gently, whisking, until sauce is thickened. Simmer for 3 minutes, stirring. Remove from heat; stir in ¾ cup of cheese. Pour sauce over cannelloni. Mix remaining cheese and bread crumbs and sprinkle over top. Bake for 30-40 minutes, or until golden. Garnish with basil sprigs.

Serves 4

TAGLIATELLE NIÇOISE

12oz dried tagliatelle
salt and freshly ground black pepper
8oz green beans, halved
4 tablespoons olive oil
1 clove garlic, crushed
2 tablespoons red or green pesto
2 tablespoons apple juice
14oz can tuna in oil, drained and flaked
4 plum tomatoes, skinned and quartered
2 tablespoons roughly chopped pitted black olives
2oz can anchovy fillets, drained and
    cut in half lengthwise
1 tablespoon chopped fresh parsley
1 tablespoon chopped fresh basil
2 eggs, hard-cooked, shelled and quartered,
    to garnish (optional)

Cook pasta in a large saucepan of lightly salted boiling water for 10-12, minutes or until just cooked or al dente. Meanwhile, cook green beans in a separate saucepan of boiling water for 5-6 minutes, or until cooked and tender. Drain well, set aside and rinse out and dry the saucepan. Heat oil in the pan, add garlic, and cook gently for 2 minutes. Whisk in pesto and apple juice and simmer gently for 1 minute. Drain pasta and return to the rinsed-out pan.

Add oil mixture and toss well to mix. Add green beans, tuna, tomatoes, olives, anchovies, chopped herbs, and salt and pepper, and toss to mix. Serve on warmed plates and garnish with egg quarters, if using. Serve with crusty French bread.

Serves 4

VARIATIONS: Use canned salmon in place of tuna. Use cooked fava beans or Italian green beans in place of green beans.

— TASTY TUNA SPAGHETTINI —

¼ cup butter
8oz leeks, washed and sliced
8oz cremini mushrooms, sliced
¼ cup all-purpose flour
1¼ cups milk
⅔ cup heavy cream
14oz can tuna in oil, drained and flaked
⅓ cup chopped pitted black olives
3 tablespoons chopped fresh parsley
good pinch of cayenne pepper
salt and freshly ground black pepper
12oz dried spaghettini
marjoram sprigs, to garnish

Melt butter in a pan, add leeks and mushrooms, and cook for 10 minutes, stirring occasionally, until soft. Add flour and cook gently for 1 minute, stirring. Remove pan from heat and gradually whisk in milk and cream, then cook, stirring continuously, until sauce is thickened and smooth. Simmer gently for 2 minutes, stirring. Stir in tuna, olives, chopped parsley, cayenne pepper, and salt and pepper, and reheat gently until very hot, stirring.

Meanwhile, cook pasta in a large saucepan of lightly salted boiling water for 10-12 minutes, or until just cooked or al dente. Drain thoroughly and serve on warmed plates. Spoon tuna sauce over pasta and garnish with marjoram sprigs. Serve with fresh crusty bread and a mixed leaf salad.

Serves 4

VARIATION: Broil or bake about 10oz fresh tuna steaks until cooked, then flake and add to sauce in place of canned tuna.

— SPICED MUSSEL LINGUINE —

1 tablespoon olive oil
1 red onion, finely chopped
1 red bell pepper, seeded and finely diced
2 cloves garlic, crushed
2 small fresh chilies, seeded and finely chopped
2 teaspoons ground coriander
2 teaspoons ground cumin
1 x 14oz can chopped tomatoes AND 1 x 8oz can
  chopped tomatoes
⅔ cup dry white wine
2 tablespoons tomato paste
salt and freshly ground black pepper
12oz cooked, shelled mussels
1lb 2oz fresh linguine
8 cooked fresh mussels in their shells
herb sprigs, to garnish

Heat oil in a saucepan, add onion, red bell pepper, garlic, and chilies, and cook for 5 minutes, stirring. Add ground spices and cook for 1 minute, stirring. Stir in chopped tomatoes, wine, tomato paste, and salt and pepper. Bring to a boil, then cook, uncovered, over a moderate heat for about 15 minutes, stirring occasionally, until sauce has thickened slightly. Stir in shelled mussels and cook for about 5 minutes, stirring occasionally, until very hot.

Meanwhile, cook pasta in a large saucepan of lightly salted boiling water for 3 minutes, or until just cooked or al dente. Drain thoroughly and serve on warmed plates. Spoon mussel sauce over pasta and garnish with fresh mussels in their shells and herb sprigs. Alternatively, toss mussel sauce and cooked pasta together before serving. Serve with warm ciabatta bread and a mixed baby leaf salad.

Serves 4

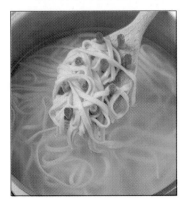

STUFFED PASTA SHELLS

16 dried conchiglioni (large pasta shells)
salt and freshly ground black pepper
3 tablespoons butter
3 shallots, finely chopped
1 red bell pepper, seeded and finely chopped
1 teaspoon grated fresh root ginger
2 x 6oz cans crab meat, drained
1 tablespoon chopped fresh cilantro
8oz mushrooms, sliced
⅔ cup dry white wine
scant 1 cup heavy cream
5 tablespoons finely grated fresh Parmesan cheese
cilantro sprigs, to garnish

Preheat oven to 375F (190C). Cook pasta in a large saucepan of lightly salted boiling water for 10 minutes, or until just cooked or al dente. Meanwhile, melt 1 tablespoon butter in a pan, add shallots, red bell pepper, and ginger, and sauté for about 5 minutes, until soft. Remove pan from heat and stir in crab meat, chopped cilantro, and salt and pepper. Set aside. Drain pasta, rinse under cold running water and drain again. Set aside. Melt remaining butter in a saucepan, and cook mushrooms over a fairly high heat for about 5 minutes, stirring occasionally, until softened.

Add wine, bring to a boil and cook over a high heat until reduced by half. Stir in cream, 2 tablespoons Parmesan, and salt and pepper, and heat gently until bubbling. Remove pan from heat and keep hot. Fill pasta shells with crab mixture. Pour mushroom sauce into a shallow ovenproof dish and place filled pasta shells on top. Sprinkle remaining Parmesan over the top. Bake for 20 minutes, or until bubbling and golden. Garnish with cilantro sprigs and serve with a mixed green salad.

Serves 4

TUNA & CORN BAKE

1 tablespoon olive oil
1 onion, finely chopped
1 yellow bell pepper, seeded and diced
2 sticks celery, finely chopped
2 zucchini, finely diced
14oz can chopped tomatoes
⅔ cup dry white wine
2 teaspoons dried Italian herb seasoning
salt and freshly ground black pepper
10oz dried penne rigate
2 x 7oz cans corn kernels, drained
14oz can tuna in brine, drained and flaked
½ cup finely grated fresh Parmesan cheese
herb sprigs, to garnish

Preheat oven to 375F (190C). Heat oil in a saucepan, add onion, yellow bell pepper, and celery, and cook for 5 minutes, stirring occasionally. Stir in zucchini, tomatoes, wine, dried herbs, and salt and pepper. Bring to a boil, then reduce heat, cover, and simmer for 10 minutes, stirring occasionally. Uncover, increase heat slightly, and cook for a further 5 minutes, or until sauce has reduced and thickened slightly. Meanwhile, cook pasta in a large saucepan of lightly salted boiling water for 10 minutes, or until just cooked or al dente. Drain and return to rinsed-out pan.

Add tomato sauce, corn, and tuna, and toss well to mix. Transfer to an ovenproof dish and sprinkle with Parmesan cheese. Bake for 20-25 minutes, or until bubbling and golden. Garnish with herb sprigs and serve with warm ciabatta bread.

Serves 4-6

VARIATIONS: Use canned salmon or cooked smoked cod or haddock in place of tuna. Use Cheddar or Gruyère cheese in place of Parmesan.

— PEPPERED SALMON FUSILLI —

2 tablespoons mixed peppercorns
3 salmon steaks, each about 6oz
juice of 1 lime
12oz crème fraîche
4 scallions, finely chopped
2oz watercress, chopped
salt and freshly ground black pepper
1lb 2oz fresh tricolore fusilli or conchiglie
dill sprigs, to garnish

Preheat broiler to medium. Crush peppercorns coarsely using a pestle and mortar, then sprinkle on to a plate. Press each salmon steak into pepper, covering both sides completely.

Put salmon steaks on a rack in a broiler pan and drizzle lime juice over. Broil for 8-10 minutes, turning once, until fish is cooked and is just beginning to flake. Skin and flake salmon, set aside and keep hot. Pour crème fraîche into a saucepan and heat gently until almost boiling. Add scallions, watercress, and salt and pepper, and cook until heated through. Stir in salmon.

Meanwhile, cook pasta in a large saucepan of lightly salted boiling water for 3 minutes, or until just cooked or al dente. Drain pasta thoroughly and return to the rinsed-out pan. Add salmon sauce and toss well to mix. Serve on warmed plates and garnish with dill sprigs. Serve with fresh soft bread rolls and a mixed leaf salad.

Serves 4

VARIATION: Use tuna steaks in place of salmon.

SPICED SHRIMP STIR-FRY

1 tablespoon cornstarch
scant ½ cup apple juice
2 tablespoons dry sherry
1 tablespoon light soy sauce
salt and freshly ground black pepper
12oz dried tomato or plain tagliatelle
1 tablespoon olive oil
6 shallots, thinly sliced
1 clove garlic, crushed
1in piece fresh root ginger, peeled and
　finely chopped
1 tablespoon Chinese 5-spice seasoning
2 carrots, cut into thin matchstick strips
2 red bell peppers, seeded and sliced
6oz snow peas
12oz cooked shelled jumbo shrimp

In a small bowl, blend cornstarch with apple
juice, sherry, soy sauce, and salt and pepper.
Set aside. Cook pasta in a large saucepan of
lightly salted boiling water for 10-12
minutes, or until just cooked or al dente.
Meanwhile, heat oil in a wok or large
skillet, add shallots, garlic, and ginger, and
stir-fry over a high heat for 1 minute.

Add Chinese 5-spice seasoning and stir-fry
for 30 seconds, then add carrots and red bell
peppers, and stir-fry for 2-3 minutes. Add
snow peas and shrimp, and stir-fry for a
further 2-3 minutes. Add cornstarch
mixture, stir until mixture thickens, then
stir-fry for a further 1-2 minutes. Drain pasta
thoroughly and add to the wok. Toss to mix,
then serve on warmed plates. Serve with a
crisp mixed leaf salad.

Serves 4

— SEAFOOD SOUFFLÉ LASAGNE —

⅓ cup butter
9 tablespoons all-purpose flour
5 cups milk
10oz skinless salmon fillet or tuna steak, diced
8oz skinless cod or haddock fillet, diced
6oz cooked peeled shrimp
8oz frozen peas
7oz can corn kernels, drained
2 tablespoons drained capers, roughly chopped
3 tablespoons chopped fresh parsley
1 tablespoon chopped fresh tarragon
salt and freshly ground black pepper
2 eggs, separated
9 no pre-cook lasagne sheets
4 tablespoons finely grated fresh Parmesan cheese
herb sprigs, to garnish

Preheat oven to 350F (180C). Put ¼ cup butter in a saucepan with ½ cup flour and 3¾ cups milk. Heat gently, whisking, until sauce is thickened and smooth. Simmer gently for 3 minutes, stirring. Add salmon or tuna, cod or haddock, shrimp, peas, corn, capers, chopped herbs, and salt and pepper and mix well. Set aside. Put remaining butter, flour, and milk in a separate saucepan. Heat gently, whisking, until sauce is thickened and smooth. Simmer gently for 3 minutes, stirring. Cool slightly, then stir in egg yolks and salt and pepper.

Whisk egg whites in a bowl until stiff, then fold them carefully into white sauce. Set aside. Spoon one-third of fish mixture into a shallow ovenproof lasagne dish. Top with three sheets of lasagne. Repeat these layers twice more. Spoon soufflé mixture over lasagne covering it completely. Sprinkle Parmesan over the top. Bake for 35-40 minutes, or until soufflé topping has risen and is golden brown. Garnish with herb sprigs and serve with cooked fresh vegetables.

Serves 4-6

— SPINACH CANNELLONI —

1½lb ripe tomatoes, skinned, seeded and chopped
2 leeks, washed and sliced
2 sticks celery, finely chopped
scant 1 cup dry white wine
2 tablespoons tomato paste
1 tablespoon mixed ground spices
salt and freshly ground black pepper
1lb 2oz fresh spinach leaves, washed
12 fresh lasagne sheets
1 cup ricotta cheese
½ teaspoon freshly grated nutmeg
2 eggs, beaten
generous ¾ cup finely grated fresh Parmesan cheese
2 teaspoons garlic paste
herb sprigs, to garnish

Preheat oven to 350F (180C). Put first 6 ingredients and salt and pepper in a saucepan and mix well. Bring to a boil, reduce heat, cover, and simmer for 20-25 minutes, stirring occasionally, until vegetables are tender. Meanwhile, put spinach in a saucepan with just the water that clings to its leaves. Cover and cook for 3-4 minutes, or until just wilted. Drain well, press out excess liquid, and chop roughly. Set aside. Cook lasagne in batches in a saucepan of lightly salted water for 2 minutes. Drain, refresh in cold water, then drain again. Set aside.

Put spinach in a bowl with ricotta, nutmeg, eggs, ½ cup Parmesan, garlic paste, and salt and pepper, and mix well. Lay lasagne out on counter and spoon some spinach mixture along long edge of each sheet. Roll lasagne to make cannelloni. Arrange cannelloni, seam-side down, in a shallow ovenproof dish. Puree tomato mixture in a blender or food processor. Pour evenly over cannelloni and bake for 30-40 minutes. Sprinkle with remaining Parmesan and garnish with herb sprigs.

Serves 4-6

— MEDITERRANEAN LASAGNE —

1 onion, sliced
1 clove garlic, crushed
1 red bell pepper, seeded and sliced
1 yellow bell pepper, seeded and sliced
1lb zucchini, sliced
12oz mushrooms, sliced
14oz can chopped tomatoes
2 teaspoons dried herbes de provence
salt and freshly ground black pepper
3 tablespoons butter
⅓ cup all-purpose flour
2½ cups milk
1 teaspoon Dijon mustard
1 cup grated pecorino or Cheddar cheese
9 no pre-cook egg lasagne sheets
¼ cup fresh Parmesan cheese, finely grated

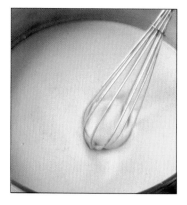

Preheat the oven to 375F (190C). Put onion, garlic, bell peppers, zucchini, mushrooms, tomatoes, dried herbs, and salt and pepper in a large saucepan, and mix well. Cover and cook for 10 minutes, stirring occasionally. Meanwhile, melt butter in a saucepan, add flour, and cook gently for 1 minute, stirring. Gradually whisk in milk and mustard, then cook, whisking continuously, until sauce is thickened and smooth. Simmer gently for 2 minutes, stirring. Remove the pan from the heat and stir in pecorino cheese, then set aside.

Spoon one-third of the vegetable mixture into an ovenproof lasagne dish and top with 3 sheets of lasagne. Repeat these layers twice more, ending with a layer of lasagne. Pour cheese sauce over the top, covering pasta completely. Sprinkle Parmesan over the top. Bake for 35-40 minutes, or until golden brown and bubbling. Serve with hot crusty garlic bread and a mixed salad.

Serves 4

RATATOUILLE BEAN BAKE

1 red onion, thinly sliced
2 cloves garlic, crushed
1 small eggplant (about 7oz), diced
2 zucchini, sliced
1 yellow bell pepper, seeded and sliced
6oz cremini mushrooms, sliced
14oz can chopped tomatoes
2 tablespoons tomato paste
4 tablespoons olive oil
2 teaspoons dried herbes de Provence
salt and freshly ground black pepper
14oz can red kidney beans, rinsed and drained
14oz can flageolet beans, rinsed and drained
10oz dried orecchiette
finely grated fresh Parmesan or mature Cheddar
  cheese, to serve

Preheat the oven to 350F (180C). Put onion, garlic, eggplant, zucchini, yellow bell pepper, mushrooms, tomatoes, tomato paste, olive oil, dried herbs, and salt and pepper in a large ovenproof dish, and stir to mix well. Cover and bake for 30 minutes. Stir in beans, cover, and bake for a further 30-45 minutes, stirring once, until vegetables are cooked and tender.

Meanwhile, cook pasta in a large saucepan of lightly salted boiling water for 12-15 minutes, or until just cooked or al dente. Drain thoroughly. Add pasta to ratatouille and toss well to mix. Serve on warmed plates and sprinkle generously with Parmesan or Cheddar cheese. Serve with fresh crusty bread.

Serves 4-6

— THREE-CHEESE MACARONI —

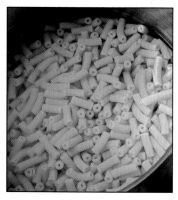

8oz dried short-cut macaroni
salt and freshly ground black pepper
¼ cup butter
½ cup all-purpose flour
generous 3 cups milk
2 teaspoons Dijon mustard
1½ cups grated Cheddar or pecorino cheese
4oz mozzarella cheese, finely diced
1 cup finely grated fresh Parmesan cheese
4 tablespoons fresh wholewheat bread crumbs
marjoram sprig, to garnish

Cook pasta in a large saucepan of lightly salted boiling water for 8-10 minutes, or until just cooked or al dente.

Meanwhile, melt butter in a separate saucepan, add flour, and cook gently for 1 minute, stirring. Gradually whisk in milk and mustard, and cook, whisking continuously, until sauce is thickened and smooth. Simmer gently for 2 minutes, stirring. Stir in Cheddar or pecorino cheese, mozzarella, ½ cup Parmesan, and salt and pepper. Drain pasta thoroughly and add to cheese sauce. Mix well, then transfer to a flameproof dish.

Preheat the broiler to high. Mix remaining Parmesan with bread crumbs and sprinkle over macaroni cheese. Broil for a few minutes or until golden brown and bubbling. Garnish with marjoram sprig, and serve with cooked fresh vegetables such as green beans and baby corn.

Serves 4

VARIATION: Top macaroni cheese with sliced tomatoes, sprinkle bread crumbs and Parmesan over the top, and broil as above.

— BROCCOLI & ZUCCHINI BAKE —

8oz dried penne rigate
salt and freshly ground black pepper
8oz small broccoli flowerets
8oz zucchini, sliced
¼ cup butter
½ cup all-purpose flour
generous 3 cups milk
⅔ cup heavy cream
1¾ cups grated mature Cheddar cheese
2 teaspoons wholegrain mustard
3 tablespoons chopped fresh parsley
2 tablespoons fresh bread crumbs
1 tablespoon sunflower seeds (optional)
parsley sprigs, to garnish

Preheat the oven to 400F (200C). Lightly grease an ovenproof dish and set aside. Cook pasta in a large saucepan of lightly salted boiling water for 10 minutes, or until just cooked or al dente. Meanwhile, cook broccoli and zucchini in a saucepan of boiling water for 3 minutes. Drain well and keep warm. Put butter, flour, milk, and cream in a saucepan and heat gently, whisking continuously, until sauce is thickened and smooth. Simmer gently for 3 minutes, stirring.

Remove pan from heat and stir in 1½ cups cheese, the mustard, chopped parsley, and salt and pepper. Drain pasta thoroughly and add to sauce with vegetables. Stir gently to mix. Transfer to prepared dish. Mix together remaining cheese, bread crumbs and sunflower seeds, if using, and sprinkle over pasta. Bake for 20 minutes, or until golden brown and bubbling. Garnish with parsley sprigs and serve with crusty French bread and a mixed dark leaf salad.

Serves 4

ITALIAN PASTA STIR-FRY

12oz dried spaghetti or bucatini
salt and freshly ground black pepper
2 tablespoons olive oil
1 onion, thinly sliced
2 cloves garlic, crushed
1 red bell pepper, seeded and sliced
1 yellow bell pepper, seeded and sliced
3 zucchini, diagonally sliced
4 plum tomatoes, seeded and chopped
⅔ cup tomato sauce
2 tablespoons chopped fresh mixed herbs
¾ cup finely grated fresh Parmesan cheese
herb sprigs, to garnish

Cook pasta in a large saucepan of lightly salted boiling water for 10-12 minutes, or until just cooked or al dente. Meanwhile, heat oil in a wok or large skillet, add onion and garlic, and stir-fry over a fairly high heat for 1 minute. Add bell peppers and zucchini and stir-fry for 3-4 minutes. Add tomatoes, tomato sauce, chopped herbs, and salt and pepper, and stir-fry for a further 1-2 minutes. Remove the pan from the heat.

Drain pasta thoroughly, add to the wok, and toss well to mix. Sprinkle Parmesan cheese over pasta and toss gently to mix. Serve on warmed plates. Garnish with herb sprigs and serve with warm focaccia bread.

Serves 4-6

VARIATIONS: Use 2 leeks, washed and sliced, or 6 shallots in place of onion. Use regular tomatoes in place of plum tomatoes.

— STUFFED ROAST BELL PEPPERS —

2 red bell peppers
2 yellow bell peppers
3 tablespoons olive oil
1 leek, washed and finely chopped
1 clove garlic, crushed
4oz mushrooms, finely chopped
6oz cooked small pasta shapes such as
   tubettini or fusillini
1 cup grated Cheddar cheese
3 plum tomatoes, chopped
3 tablespoons chopped fresh basil
salt and freshly ground black pepper
basil sprigs, to garnish

Preheat the oven to 350F (180C). Cut bell peppers in half lengthwise, remove cores and seeds, and place bell pepper halves on a baking sheet, hollow-side up. Set aside. Heat 1 tablespoon oil in a saucepan, add leek, garlic, and mushrooms, and cook gently for 5 minutes, stirring occasionally. Remove the pan from the heat and stir in cooked pasta, cheese, tomatoes, chopped basil, and salt and pepper, and mix well.

Spoon mixture into bell pepper halves and drizzle with remaining oil. Bake for 35-40 minutes, or until filling is golden and bubbling. Garnish with basil sprigs, and serve with crusty French bread and a mixed baby leaf salad.

Serves 4

VARIATIONS: Use Red Leicester cheese in place of Cheddar. Use zucchini in place of mushrooms.

CHEESE GNOCCHI

2 x 14oz cans cherry tomatoes
1 red onion, finely chopped
2 cloves garlic, crushed
3 tablespoons tomato paste
1 teaspoon fennel seeds, crushed
1 teaspoon dried chili flakes, crushed
salt and freshly ground black pepper
1½lb peeled potatoes, diced
¾ cup finely grated fresh Parmesan cheese
½ cup finely grated pecorino cheese
2 tablespoons butter
1 egg, beaten
1¼ cups all-purpose flour
herb sprigs, to garnish

Put tomatoes, onion, garlic, tomato paste, fennel seeds, chili flakes, and salt and pepper in a saucepan. Bring to a boil, then reduce heat and simmer, uncovered, for 25-30 minutes, stirring occasionally, until sauce is thick and pulpy. Meanwhile, make the gnocchi. Cook potatoes in a saucepan of boiling water for 10-15 minutes, or until tender. Drain well, then return to the pan and mash until smooth. Add the Parmesan and pecorino cheeses, butter, egg, and salt and pepper, and beat until smooth and well mixed.

Add half the flour and mix well, then gradually add remaining flour, until dough is smooth and slightly sticky. Divide in half and roll each piece into a long thin sausage shape, then cut into 2.5-3cm (1-1¼in) lengths. Chill for 30 minutes. Cook gnocchi in batches in a large pan of lightly salted boiling water for 4-5 minutes. Remove from pan using a slotted spoon, drain well and keep hot. Serve on warmed plates with sauce spooned over. Garnish with herb sprigs.

Serves 4-6

—— TOMATO & BRIE BAKE ——

1lb cherry tomatoes, halved
3 tablespoons olive oil
4 shallots, thinly sliced
2 cloves garlic, crushed
8oz button mushrooms, sliced
1lb 2oz fresh radiatore
salt and freshly ground black pepper
generous 1 cup mascarpone
4 tablespoons chopped fresh basil
8oz Brie, rind removed and cheese diced (weight
    without rind)
⅓ cup finely grated fresh Parmesan cheese
basil sprigs, to garnish

Preheat oven to 350F (180C). Put tomatoes, cut-side up in a single layer in a large shallow ovenproof dish and drizzle 2 tablespoons oil over. Bake for 10 minutes. Meanwhile, heat remaining oil in a saucepan, add shallots, garlic, and mushrooms, and cook for 5 minutes, stirring occasionally. Cook pasta in a large saucepan of lightly salted boiling water for about 4 minutes, until just cooked or al dente. Drain thoroughly and return to the rinsed-out saucepan.

Add shallot mixture, mascarpone, chopped basil, and salt and pepper, and toss well to mix. Add tomatoes and their juices and stir gently to mix, then gently fold in the Brie. Transfer mixture to an ovenproof dish. Sprinkle Parmesan over the top. Bake for about 20 minutes, or until the top is golden. Garnish with basil sprigs and serve with a mixed green salad.

Serves 6

COUNTRY-STYLE PASTA

2 tablespoons olive oil
3oz sun-dried tomatoes in oil
  (drained weight), roughly chopped
6oz bottled roasted mixed bell peppers
  (drained weight), cut into thin strips
2 cloves garlic, crushed
10fl oz tomato sauce
1lb 2oz fresh riccioli
salt and freshly ground black pepper
4 tablespoons chopped fresh basil
½ cup finely grated fresh Parmesan cheese
basil sprigs, to garnish

Heat oil in a saucepan, add sun-dried tomatoes, bell peppers, and garlic, and cook for 3 minutes, stirring occasionally. Add tomato sauce and bring to a boil, then simmer gently, uncovered, for 5 minutes, stirring occasionally. Meanwhile, cook pasta in a large saucepan of lightly salted boiling water for 3 minutes, or until just cooked or al dente. Drain the pasta thoroughly and return to the rinsed-out saucepan.

Stir chopped basil, and salt and pepper into sauce, then add to pasta and toss well to mix. Serve on warmed plates and sprinkle with Parmesan. Garnish with basil sprigs and serve with hot crusty garlic bread.

Serves 4

VARIATIONS: Use oil from the jar of sun-dried tomatoes in place of olive oil. Use 2-3 tablespoons chopped fresh cilantro in place of basil.

ZUCCHINI FRITTATA

¼ cup dried short-cut macaroni
salt and freshly ground black pepper
¼ cup butter
1 onion, chopped
1 clove garlic, crushed
2 zucchini, thinly sliced
1 small red bell pepper, seeded and thinly sliced
4oz mushrooms, sliced
6 eggs
2 teaspoons dried Italian herb seasoning
1 cup finely grated fresh Parmesan cheese
herb sprigs, to garnish

Cook pasta in a large saucepan of lightly salted boiling water for 10 minutes, or until just cooked or al dente.

Meanwhile, melt butter in a large non-stick skillet, add onion, garlic, zucchini, red bell pepper, and mushrooms, and cook for 8-10 minutes, stirring occasionally, until softened. Drain pasta thoroughly, then add to vegetables and stir to mix. In a bowl, beat eggs with dried herbs and salt and pepper, then stir in ¾ cup Parmesan. Pour egg mixture over vegetables and pasta, and stir briefly to mix, spreading the mixture out evenly in the pan.

Cook over a medium heat, without stirring, until eggs are beginning to set and frittata is golden brown underneath. Preheat broiler to medium. Sprinkle remaining cheese over the top of the frittata, then broil until top is lightly browned. Cut into wedges to serve and garnish with herb sprigs. Serve with warm ciabatta bread and a mixed dark leaf salad.

Serves 4-6

BAKED MUSHROOM TORTELLONI

⅓ cup butter
1 small red onion, finely chopped
1 clove garlic, crushed
8oz button mushrooms, halved
4oz mixed fresh wild mushrooms, sliced
⅓ cup all-purpose flour
2 cups milk
⅔ cup light cream
4oz Dolcelatte cheese, diced
1lb fresh spinach and ricotta tortelloni
salt and freshly ground black pepper
3 tablespoons chopped fresh flat-leaf parsley
3 tablespoons fresh bread crumbs

Preheat the oven to 400F (200C). Melt 2 tablespoons butter in a saucepan, add onion, garlic, and mushrooms, and sauté for 5 minutes. Remove vegetables from the pan using a slotted spoon and place in a sieve over a bowl. Set aside to drain. Add remaining butter to pan and heat until melted. Add flour and cook for 1 minute, stirring. Gradually whisk in milk and cream, then cook, whisking continuously, until sauce is thickened and smooth. Simmer gently for 2 minutes, stirring, then add Dolcelatte cheese and stir until melted.

Meanwhile, cook pasta in a large saucepan of lightly salted boiling water for 4 minutes, or until just cooked or al dente. Drain thoroughly and return to rinsed-out pan. Add mushroom mixture to pasta with 2 tablespoons chopped parsley, cheese sauce, and salt and pepper; toss well to mix. Transfer to an ovenproof dish. Mix remaining parsley and bread crumbs together and sprinkle over pasta. Bake for 20-25 minutes, or until golden brown and bubbling.

Serves 4

—BELL PEPPER & LEEK GRATIN—

4 bell peppers (2 red and 2 yellow)
12oz dried wholewheat fusilli
salt and freshly ground black pepper
¼ cup butter
4 leeks, washed and sliced
1 fresh red chili, seeded and finely chopped
6 tablespoons crème fraîche
1 cup grated Emmental cheese
2 tablespoons fresh bread crumbs
1 teaspoon paprika
herb sprigs, to garnish

Preheat broiler to high. Halve bell peppers lengthwise and put them, cut-side down, on rack in a broiler pan.

Broil for 10-15 minutes, or until skins are blackened and charred. Remove from the heat, cover bell peppers with a clean damp dish towel and set aside to cool. Once cool, remove and discard skin, cores, and seeds from bell peppers and cut flesh into strips. Set aside. Cook pasta in a large saucepan of lightly salted boiling water for 10 minutes, or until just cooked or al dente. Meanwhile, melt butter in a pan, add leeks, and chili, and cook gently for 8-10 minutes, stirring occasionally, until softened. Add bell pepper strips and cook briefly.

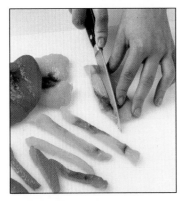

Drain pasta thoroughly and return to the rinsed-out pan. Add vegetables, crème fraîche, and salt and pepper, and toss well to mix. Transfer mixture to a shallow flameproof dish. Mix together cheese, bread crumbs, and paprika, and sprinkle over the top. Broil for a few minutes, or until golden brown on top and bubbling. Garnish with herb sprigs and serve with crusty French bread.

Serves 4-6

—— PANCETTA BEAN SALAD ——

12oz frozen baby fava beans
12oz fresh penne rigate
salt and freshly ground black pepper
1 tablespoon olive oil
10oz pancetta, finely diced
1 clove garlic, crushed
1 bunch scallions, chopped diagonally
1 yellow bell pepper, seeded and diced
scant 1 cup tomato sauce
2 tablespoons chopped fresh basil
basil sprigs, to garnish

Cook beans and pasta in a pan of lightly salted boiling water for 5 minutes, or until beans are tender and pasta is just cooked or al dente.

Drain thoroughly, set aside, and keep warm. Meanwhile, heat oil in a wok or large skillet, add pancetta and stir-fry for 3-4 minutes. Add garlic, scallions, and yellow bell pepper and stir-fry for 2-3 minutes, until just tender. Add tomato sauce, and salt and pepper, and stir-fry until hot and bubbling.

Add cooked fava beans, pasta, and chopped basil, and stir-fry to mix. Serve on warmed plates and garnish with basil sprigs. Serve with warm crusty garlic and herb bread or ciabatta bread.

Serves 4

VARIATIONS: Use diced smoked bacon or diced chorizo in place of pancetta. Use chopped fresh cilantro or flat-leaf parsley in place of basil.

– CHORIZO & CHICKPEA SALAD –

8oz dried fusilli
salt and freshly ground black pepper
14oz can chickpeas, rinsed and drained
8oz baby plum tomatoes, halved
1 orange or yellow bell pepper, seeded and diced
4oz sugar-snap peas, chopped
2oz arugula leaves
1 bunch spring scallions, chopped
8oz cooked chorizo, thinly sliced
6 tablespoons tomato juice or tomato sauce
2 tablespoons olive oil
2 teaspoons balsamic vinegar
1 tablespoon chopped fresh mixed herbs
½ teaspoon light soft brown sugar

Cook pasta in a large saucepan of lightly salted boiling water for 10-12 minutes, or until just cooked or al dente. Drain, rinse under cold running water, then drain again thoroughly. Set aside to cool completely. Put cold pasta in a large bowl with chickpeas, chorizo, tomatoes, orange or yellow bell pepper, sugar-snap peas, arugula leaves and scallions, and toss well to mix.

Put the tomato juice or tomato sauce, oil, vinegar, chopped herbs, sugar, and salt and pepper in a small bowl and whisk together until thoroughly mixed. Pour over pasta salad and toss gently to mix. Serve with crusty bread rolls.

Serves 4-6

VARIATIONS: Use cannellini beans in place of chickpeas. Use cucumber or radishes in place of sugar-snap peas.

— CHICKEN & AVOCADO SALAD —

12oz fresh radiatore
salt and freshly ground black pepper
4oz mixed salad leaves
2oz watercress
1oz cress
8oz skinless, boneless cooked chicken, diced
1 ripe avocado
1 tablespoon lemon juice
8 tablespoons mayonnaise
2 tablespoons chopped fresh parsley
1 teaspoon finely grated lemon zest
parsley sprigs, to garnish

Cook pasta in a large saucepan of lightly salted boiling water for 4 minutes, or until just cooked or al dente.

Drain, rinse under cold running water, then drain again thoroughly. Set aside to cool completely. Put salad leaves, watercress, and cress in a bowl and toss to mix. Divide salad evenly between four plates and set aside. Put cold pasta in a bowl with chicken and stir to mix. Peel, stone and dice avocado, toss it with lemon juice, then add to pasta mixture. Toss to mix.

Put mayonnaise, parsley, lemon zest and salt and pepper in a small bowl and mix well. Spoon dressing over pasta mixture and toss gently to mix. Spoon some chicken and pasta mixture into the center of each plate of salad. Garnish with parsley sprigs and serve with crusty French bread.

Serves 4

VARIATIONS: Use arugula leaves in place of watercress. Use cooked turkey in place of chicken.

– WARM DUCK FARFALLE SALAD –

8oz dried farfalle
salt and freshly ground black pepper
3oz mixed salad leaves
8 scallions, chopped
1 ripe mango, peeled, stoned, and diced or
  thinly sliced
4 tablespoons olive oil
1 tablespoon white wine vinegar
1 teaspoon honey
2 tablespoons chopped fresh cilantro
1 tablespoon sesame oil
8oz skinless, boneless duck breast,
  cut into thin strips
4oz mange-tout, trimmed
1-2 tablespoons toasted sesame seeds, to garnish
  (optional)

Cook pasta in a large saucepan of lightly
salted boiling water for 10-12 minutes, or
until just cooked or al dente. Meanwhile,
put salad leaves, scallions, and mango in a
large bowl and toss to mix. Set aside. Put
olive oil, vinegar, honey, chopped cilantro,
and salt and pepper in a small bowl and
whisk together until thoroughly mixed. Set
aside.

Heat sesame oil in a wok or large skillet, add
duck and stir-fry over a high heat for 3-4
minutes. Add mange-tout and stir-fry for a
further 1-2 minutes, or until duck is cooked
and tender. Drain pasta thoroughly and add
to salad leaves with hot duck mixture. Toss
gently to mix. Give dressing a quick whisk,
then pour it over salad and toss to mix.
Spoon on to plates and garnish with a
sprinkling of sesame seeds, if liked. Serve
with soft bread rolls.

Serves 4

— SMOKED MACKEREL SALAD —

12oz fresh strozzapretti
8oz frozen peas
salt and freshly ground black pepper
7oz can corn kernels, drained
1 red bell pepper, seeded and finely diced
1 bunch scallions, chopped
8oz skinless smoked mackerel fillets, flaked
6 tablespoons mayonnaise
4 tablespoons plain yogurt
1 tablespoon creamed horseradish
3 tablespoons chopped fresh chives

Cook pasta and peas in a large saucepan of lightly salted boiling water for 4 minutes, or until pasta is just cooked or al dente.

Drain, rinse under cold running water, then drain again thoroughly. Set aside to cool completely. Put cold pasta, peas, corn, red bell pepper, and scallions in a large bowl and toss to mix. Add smoked mackerel and toss gently to mix.

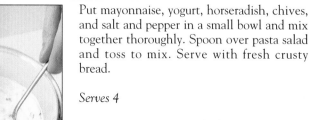

Put mayonnaise, yogurt, horseradish, chives, and salt and pepper in a small bowl and mix together thoroughly. Spoon over pasta salad and toss to mix. Serve with fresh crusty bread.

Serves 4

VARIATIONS: Use smoked trout fillets in place of mackerel. Use chopped fresh parsley in place of chives. Use 1 sweet white onion, finely chopped, in place of scallions.

——— SPICY SEAFOOD SALAD ———

8oz dried spirali
salt and freshly ground black pepper
6oz mushrooms, thinly sliced
2oz watercress, roughly chopped
9oz cherry tomatoes, halved
2 tablespoons olive oil
2 cloves garlic, crushed
1 tablespoon Cajun seasoning
14oz frozen mixed seafood, defrosted
6 tablespoons tomato sauce
2 tablespoons dry sherry
1 tablespoon light soy sauce
1 tablespoon tomato paste
herb sprigs, to garnish

Cook pasta in a large saucepan of lightly salted boiling water for 10-12 minutes, or until just cooked or al dente. Meanwhile, put mushrooms, watercress, and cherry tomatoes in a salad bowl and stir to mix. Set aside. Heat oil in a wok or large skillet, add garlic and Cajun seasoning, and stir-fry over a fairly high heat for 30 seconds. Add seafood and stir-fry for about 5 minutes, or until cooked.

Mix together the tomato sauce, sherry, soy sauce, tomato paste, and salt and pepper. Add to the wok and stir-fry until hot and bubbling. Drain pasta thoroughly, add to the wok and stir-fry to mix. Add to the salad bowl and toss well to mix. Garnish with herb sprigs and serve with hot crusty garlic bread.

Serves 4

VARIATIONS: Use fresh oyster mushrooms in place of regular mushrooms. Use arugula leaves in place of watercress.

LAYERED PASTA SALAD

8oz dried farfalle tricolore
salt and freshly ground black pepper
6 tablespoons olive oil
3 tablespoons pesto (basil sauce)
14oz can pink salmon, drained, boned, and flaked
½ cucumber, sliced
1 large beefsteak tomato, sliced
1 bunch scallions, finely chopped
1 yellow bell pepper, seeded and finely diced
4oz sugar-snap peas, chopped
herb sprigs, to garnish

Cook pasta in a large saucepan of lightly salted boiling water for 10-12 minutes, or until just cooked or al dente.

Drain, rinse under cold running water, drain again thoroughly and set aside to cool completely. Put oil, pesto, and salt and pepper in a bowl and whisk together until thoroughly mixed. Add cold pasta and toss well to mix. Add salmon and stir gently to mix. Put one-third of salmon pasta in a glass serving bowl. Arrange cucumber and tomato slices over pasta.

Top with half of remaining salmon pasta to cover cucumber and tomato slices completely. Mix scallions, yellow bell pepper, and sugar-snap peas together and scatter over pasta. Top with the remaining salmon pasta, covering vegetables completely. Cover and chill for about 1 hour before serving. Garnish with herb sprigs and serve with mini soft bread rolls.

Serves 6

— FOUR-BEAN PASTA MEDLEY —

8oz dried tricolore or wholewheat fusilli
salt and freshly ground black pepper
4oz French beans, halved
6oz frozen baby fava beans
14oz can cannellini beans, rinsed and drained
7oz can red kidney beans, rinsed and drained
1 red bell pepper, seeded and diced
1 small sweet white onion, thinly sliced
4oz button mushrooms, sliced
generous ½ cup tomato sauce or tomato juice
2 tablespoons olive oil
1 tablespoon balsamic vinegar
1 clove garlic, crushed
2 tablespoons chopped fresh cilantro
baby spinach leaves or Belgian endive leaves, to serve

Cook pasta in a large saucepan of lightly salted boiling water for 10-12 minutes, or until just cooked or al dente. Meanwhile, cook French beans in a separate saucepan of boiling water for 2 minutes, add fava beans, return to a boil, and boil for a further 3-4 minutes, or until beans are cooked and tender. Drain pasta and beans, rinse under cold running water, and drain again thoroughly. Set aside to cool completely.

Put cold pasta and cooked beans in a large salad bowl, add canned beans, red bell pepper, onion, and mushrooms and toss well to mix. Put tomato sauce or tomato juice, oil, vinegar, garlic, chopped cilantro, and salt and pepper in a small bowl and whisk together until thoroughly mixed. Pour over pasta salad and toss well to mix. Serve on a bed of spinach or Belgian endive leaves. Serve with warm ciabatta bread.

Serves 4-6

INDEX